THE NEW BOOK OF
WAFFLES AND PIZZELLES

Donna Rathmell German

BRISTOL PUBLISHING ENTERPRISES

San Leandro, California

A **nitty gritty**® Cookbook

Printed in the United States of America.

ISBN: 1-55867-278-8

Cover design: Frank J. Paredes
Cover photography: John A. Benson
Food stylist: Susan Devaty
Illustrator: Caryn Leschen

CONTENTS

BE CREATIVE WITH WAFFLES AND PIZZELLES

The popularity of pizzelle makers has inspired me to add information and recipes for the crisp Italian cookie to this revision of my bestselling *Waffles* book. Pizzelles are thin, wafer-like cookies with wonderful lacy patterns, baked in special pizzelle makers, in waffle irons that can be converted into pizzelle makers, or with special pizzelle irons that were traditionally used on the stovetop. Look for pizzelle recipes and complete directions beginning on page 109, and for pizzelle fillings beginning on page 143.

While most people think about using a waffle iron on a leisurely day (such as Sunday) for fresh waffles with syrup and maybe even fresh berries, the fact is that waffles can actually be quite a diverse food for any day of the week. For instance, try any of your favorite creamed chicken or beef dishes over a whole grain waffle for an absolute treat and change-of-pace supper. Top a corn waffle with chili for a delicious meal-in-minutes. Any dish which would normally be served over rice or noodles may be served with waffles — imagine beef Stroganoff over a whole wheat waffle or a Welsh rarebit served with a ham or meat waffle! We enjoy whole grain waffles with turkey soup. You can even use waffles in place of bread when making your favorite sandwiches.

Additions to waffles are unlimited; try waffles with fruits, vegetables, nuts, chocolate, spices, cheeses and even meats. The recipes in this book will serve as a springboard for your imagination in waffle making.

Your first reaction may be to avoid waffles made with yeast as the leavening agent instead of the more common baking powder. Proofing the yeast is not as difficult as you may think and it is, in fact, a quicker way to get waffles to the table in the morning, as most of the batter is prepared the evening before. Give it a try!

Waffle toppings themselves can be varied. Don't limit yourself to maple syrup — try waffles with applesauce, fresh fruit, yogurt, whipped cream or any of the delicious toppings provided for you in this book.

If you love waffles but don't have the time to prepare them in the morning before you're on your way to work or school, try making them on the weekend. They can be cooled and then heated before serving. Or freeze them and then heat them in your toaster or oven (350° for 5 minutes or so). In this way you can enjoy home-made waffles, hassle-free, on the run.

Waffle irons, like sandwich makers, can also be used to cook eggs. My children love their "waffled eggs" and consider them to be a real treat. Use your waffle iron to make an interesting French toast — great for brunch entertaining, as it "dresses up" the meal. You can even use your waffle iron to heat up a regular sandwich, giving it an interesting waffled texture. I would suggest creamy-type fillings for this as opposed to meat fillings.

QUESTIONS AND ANSWERS ABOUT WAFFLE MAKING

What is the difference between a pancake batter and a waffle batter?

A waffle batter is usually a little thinner than a similar pancake batter. It will have more melted butter or vegetable oil than a pancake batter so that the resulting waffles will not stick to the iron itself. In addition, a waffle batter may have more eggs and/or sugar than pancake batter.

Can I use a favorite pancake batter in my waffle iron?

With some adaptations, a pancake batter can be used as a waffle batter. I would recommend either doubling the amount of fat (melted butter, margarine or vegetable oil) or using 3 to 4 tbs. of the fat (4 tbs. equals ¼ cup). In addition to the fat adjustment, you should beat the egg white until stiff and fold in at the very end of your batter preparation for a fluffier waffle. If there is no egg called for in your pancake recipe, use one egg per cup of flour. While this is a general rule of thumb, it may take some experimenting with your recipe so be sure to keep notes for the next time.

Can I use these waffle recipes for pancakes?

Yes, again with some minor modifications. I would recommend cutting the fat (melted butter, margarine or vegetable oil) in half. For thinner pancakes use a little extra liquid and for thicker pancakes use a little extra flour. The egg may or may not be separated and the white beaten and folded in at the end — that is your preference. The beaten egg white adds fluffiness to the results. Ladle the batter onto a hot griddle or frying pan and cook until bubbles appear. Turn the pancake over and cook until done (a golden color).

How much batter should I use for each waffle?

Pour or ladle about $1/3$ to $1/2$ cup (follow the guidelines provided by the manufacturer of your machine) of the batter into the middle of your hot, seasoned waffle iron. Cook waffles for 2 to 5 minutes or until golden brown and done.

What is the difference between a Belgian waffle and other waffles?

A Belgian waffle has deeper, thicker pockets which is the result, purely, of the type of waffle iron used. A Scandinavian waffle is usually heart-shaped, again, from the type of waffle iron. All recipes in this book will work in any of these different types of waffle irons.

The waffles sometimes stick. What should I do? It's hard to clean the iron.

Follow manufacturer's guidelines for treating or seasoning the iron. If no information is available, season it by brushing melted butter, margarine or vegetable oil onto the cooking area in order to prevent sticking.

How do I know when the waffle is completely baked?

The waffle iron will stop steaming and will be opened easily. If there is any resistance to opening the iron, wait another half-minute or so and then try again.

Should the ingredients be at room temperature when I make the batter?

With the exception of the egg and melted butter, all other ingredients can be taken directly from the refrigerator. You may, in fact, actually have better results if the ingredients are cool as the cooler temperatures restrict the development of gluten in the flour. In other words, there is a lesser probability of overbeating the batter if the ingredients are cooler.

Some recipes result in thin batters and others are thicker. Is this normal?

Yes. A thin batter will generally result in a tender waffle. A thick, rich batter will result in a crisp outside and a tender inside. Both are delicious.

Is it possible to freeze leftover waffles?

Absolutely! Any homemade waffle may be frozen and reheated just as you would a purchased frozen waffle. Simply allow the waffle to cool on a wire rack (I use the racks in the cold oven as an easy, out-of-the-way place). When the waffle is completely cool, wrap in plastic or a plastic bag and freeze. Remove the frozen waffles and heat in your toaster, toaster oven or your conventional oven (350° for about 5 minutes). It is just as easy as the purchased variety but infinitely better and contains the ingredients you have decided you want or need.

Can these recipes be made more dietetic?

To adapt any recipes in this book to diet recipes, you may try the following:

1. Increase the liquid (milk, juice, fruit puree) by about 2 tbs. This is to replace liquid lost by decreasing melted butter (or vegetable oil). If decreasing a sugar substitute such as honey or molasses, you may want to increase the liquid a little more.

2. Decrease the fat (butter, margarine or vegetable oil) to about 1 tbs. Due to the lessened fat, make sure your waffle iron is well seasoned; otherwise the waffles may have a tendency to stick to the iron.

3. Decrease sugar, honey or molasses to $1/2$ to $1 1/2$ tsp., or to taste. If decreasing honey or molasses, you may need to increase the liquid (see above) by another tablespoon or so.

4. Sugar substitutes such as NutraSweet, etc., generally cannot be used in recipes which are baked. If using a substitute such as fructose, use about $1/3$ the amount of sugar (which includes honey or molasses) given. For example,

if you are cutting the sugar to 1 tsp., use $^1/_3$ tsp. fructose. Fructose is available at your local health food store.

Is it really necessary to separate and beat the egg when making waffles?

The stiffly beaten egg white folded into the batter helps make the waffles tender and fluffy. Waffles without the beaten egg are less tender and fluffy but may still be delicious. If you decide not to beat the egg and are happy with the results, by all means do so.

What should I do if the batter looks too thin?

If the batter looks too thin and runny, add a few tablespoons to $^1/_4$ cup flour. Too thin a batter will result in a limp waffle. However, keep in mind that a waffle batter is a relatively thin, pourable batter. You don't, however, want it too thin so that it just runs between the iron's grids.

What should I do if the waffles seem limp?

This could be due to not cooking long enough or too much liquid in the batter. Different flours and grains absorb moisture at varying levels. While the recipes usually give one specific amount, some minor adjustments may be required. Add flour one or two tablespoons at a time. You should never need to add more than $^1/_4$ cup (4 tbs.) flour as the ratio of flour to water could be jeopardized. Up to $^1/_4$ cup, however, is generally safe. I find that oats, in particular, often require additional flour to be added.

What should I do if the waffles are tough and hard?

This is probably the result of overbeating the batter. The batter should only be mixed until the ingredients are just blended. It will be a lumpy batter but the lumps will bake out. It might help to use milk or juice which is cold instead of at room temperature.

It could also be that the waffles are being overcooked. Waffles are usually cooked when the steam stops and/or when the waffle iron is easily opened.

Can I use your recipes with self-rising flour?

Absolutely. If at least ¾ cup of all-purpose flour is called for, substitute self-rising flour, and omit salt and baking powder from the recipe.

I need to make waffles for a crowd. How can I do that with these recipes?

All of the recipes in this book can easily be doubled.

What should I do if the waffles are pulling apart or taking a long time to cook?

Probably the waffle iron has not been preheated properly and/or the iron is being opened too soon. Make sure the iron is preheated properly and do not open it during the first minute or two of baking — definitely not before the steaming stops.

What are some other serving suggestions for waffles?

Most people equate waffles with breakfast or brunch using a syrup. There are several different ways to vary the serving of waffles:

1. Serve basic or whole grain/cereal waffles as a base for any food which would be served with rice or noodles.
2. Serve waffles with ice cream, whipped cream or creme fraiche for dessert. Fresh fruit could be served also.
3. Use waffles as the bread for sandwiches. I would recommend using a basic or whole grain waffle for this.
4. Vary the toppings used: see *Toppings*, page 133, for ideas.
5. Waffles can also be used as a base for pizza. Top with pizza sauce, grated mozzarella and other toppings if desired; place under a broiler until cheese melts.

What are some other uses for my waffle iron?

Many people use their waffle irons to make French toast. It's an easy, hot breakfast food. The resulting French toast has the expected waffle pattern for holding favorite syrups or other toppings. Some batter ideas for French toast (about 2 slices) include:

Regular French Toast

1 egg, beaten
2–3 tbs. milk or cream
dash cinnamon or nutmeg

Orange French Toast

1 egg, beaten
1–1 1/2 tbs. orange juice
1–1 1/2 tbs. milk
1/8 tsp. orange peel

Eggnog French Toast

1/4–1/3 cup eggnog
dash cinnamon or nutmeg, optional

Combine the given ingredients and place in a bowl which is about the same shape and size as your bread. Let the bread sit in the mixture for a minute or so on each side so that it soaks up the mixture (as opposed to just dipping it in). Place the bread in the preheated waffle iron and heat for 2 to 3 minutes or until golden brown.

In addition to French toast, some people make delicious, interesting sandwiches in their waffle irons. Use a sandwich filling which is creamy as opposed to those with meats, cheeses or vegetables. For example, use fillings similar in texture to peanut butter and jelly, cream cheese and chutney, deviled ham or tuna and mayonnaise. Place your filled sandwich in the waffle maker and heat for about 2 to 3 minutes. The resulting sandwich will have the waffle imprints, making it an interesting sandwich to serve and eat. (Of course if you enjoy hot sandwiches of unlimited varieties, you may use a sandwich maker which is so designed. See my book, *The Sandwich Maker Cookbook*, for about 200 hot sandwich ideas).

Cook bacon in your waffle iron along with your waffles, French toast or regular toast. Simply place on top of the waffle batter (French toast or even plain bread) a single piece of bacon which has been cut into two or three equal pieces. Heat in the waffle iron for about 3 minutes. Serve with your favorite syrup or topping. Note that the bacon drippings cook into the waffle, so make sure you allow it to cook long enough. Otherwise the results will be greasy.

You can even cook scrambled eggs in your waffle iron. Make sure that the iron itself is well seasoned. Cook scrambled eggs with cheese or well diced, cooked meats such as bacon, turkey, ham or even ground beef. The eggs should cook until well set, about 2 to 3 minutes.

WHITE FLOUR, CHEESE AND MEAT WAFFLES

13	Basic Waffle
14	Basic Waffle – Cake Flour
14	Malted Milk Waffles
15	"Diet" Waffles
16	Sweet Butter Waffles
17	Honey Waffles
18	Buttermilk Waffles
19	Eggnog Waffles
20	Sweet Cream Waffles
20	Lemon Cream Waffles
21	Maple Waffles
22	Coconut Chocolate Chip Waffles
22	Butterscotch Waffles
23	White Chocolate Waffles
24	Cottage Cheese Waffles
24	Yogurt or Ricotta Waffles
25	Sour Cream Waffles
26	Potato Waffles
27	Bacon Waffles
27	Cheddar Cheese and Bacon Waffles
27	Cheddar Cheese Waffles
28	Meat Waffles
28	Italian Sausage Waffles
28	Country Sausage Waffles
29	Western Waffles
30	Mexican Waffles
31	Greek Cheese and Spinach Waffles

BASIC WAFFLE

This basic recipe makes a wonderful, light and fluffy waffle.

1 egg, room temperature and separated
1 cup all-purpose flour
1 tsp. baking powder
1/8 tsp. salt
1 tbs. sugar
3/4 cup milk
1/4 cup butter or margarine, melted and cooled

Beat egg white in a small bowl until stiff and set aside. Mix together dry ingredients and set aside. Combine egg yolk, milk and melted butter. Add to dry ingredients, mixing until just blended. Fold in beaten egg white until just mixed. Do not overbeat batter.

BASIC WAFFLE — CAKE FLOUR

The cake flour adds extra fluffiness to this basic waffle.

1 egg, room temperature and separated
1 1/4 cups cake flour
1 tsp. baking powder
1/8 tsp. salt
1 tbs. sugar
2/3 cup milk
1/4 cup butter or margarine, melted and cooled

Beat egg white in a small bowl until stiff and set aside. Mix together dry ingredients and set aside. Combine egg yolk, milk and melted butter. Add to dry ingredients, mixing until just blended. Fold in beaten egg white until just mixed. Do not overbeat batter.

Variation: MALTED MILK WAFFLES
Add 3 tbs. malted milk powder for unique flavoring; it's great with ice cream.

"DIET" WAFFLES

Even those of us who are constantly battling the bulge deserve waffles as a treat. Here is a relatively low-calorie recipe.

1 egg, room temperature and
  separated, or ¼ cup egg substitute
1 cup all-purpose flour
1 tsp. baking powder

½ tsp. sugar
⅛ tsp. salt
9 oz. skim milk (= 1 cup plus 2 tbs.)
1 tbs. margarine or butter, melted

If using an egg, beat egg white in a small bowl until stiff and set aside. Mix together dry ingredients and set aside. Combine egg yolk, milk and melted butter. Add to dry ingredients, mixing until just blended. Fold in beaten egg white until just mixed. Do not overbeat batter.

If using egg substitute, mix together dry ingredients and set aside. Combine egg substitute, milk and melted butter. Add to dry ingredients, mixing until just blended. As the amount of butter is significantly decreased from the normal amount, make sure that the waffle iron is well seasoned. You may use a nonstick spray unless specified by the manufacturer's directions.

Note: If you wish to try to adapt any recipe in this book to be more dietetic, please see suggestions on page 6.

SWEET BUTTER WAFFLES

Wow! Delicious, sweet, rich waffles for a decadent start to the day. Not meant for those days when you're counting calories.

1 egg, room temperature and separated
1 cup all-purpose flour
1 tsp. baking powder
1/8 tsp. salt
2 tbs. sugar
2/3 cup milk, room temperature
6 tbs. butter or margarine, melted and cooled

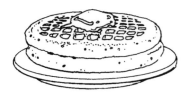

Beat egg white in a small bowl until stiff and set aside. Mix together dry ingredients and set aside. Combine egg yolk, milk and melted butter. Add to dry ingredients, mixing until just blended. Fold in beaten egg white until just mixed. Do not overbeat batter.

HONEY WAFFLES

Here is a sweet variation on a basic waffle. For a real treat, serve with plain honey, honey spread or any of the honey toppings provided in Toppings, *page 133.*

1 egg, room temperature and separated
1 cup all-purpose flour
1 tsp. baking powder
$1/8$ tsp. salt
$2/3$ cup milk
2 tbs. honey
$1/4$ cup butter or margarine, melted and cooled

Beat egg white in a small bowl until stiff and set aside. Mix together dry ingredients and set aside. Combine egg yolk, milk, honey and melted butter. Add to dry ingredients, mixing until just blended. Fold in beaten egg white until just mixed. Do not overbeat batter.

BUTTERMILK WAFFLES

This recipe makes a relatively low-calorie waffle. The thick batter rises well and makes a quite delicious waffle.

1 egg, room temperature and separated
1 cup all-purpose flour
1 tsp. baking powder
1/8 tsp. baking soda
1/8 tsp. salt
1 tsp. sugar
1 cup buttermilk
2 tbs. butter, melted and cooled

Beat egg white in a small bowl until stiff and set aside. Mix together dry ingredients and set aside. Combine egg yolk, buttermilk and melted butter. Add to dry ingredients, mixing until just blended. Fold in beaten egg white until just mixed. Do not overbeat batter.

18   WHITE FLOUR, CHEESE AND MEAT WAFFLES

EGGNOG WAFFLES

Try this for a tasty holiday-season treat. It makes a relatively thick batter.

1 egg, room temperature and separated
1 cup all-purpose flour
1 tsp. baking powder
1/8 tsp. salt
1/8 tsp. cinnamon
1/16 tsp. nutmeg
1 tbs. brown sugar
3/4 cup eggnog
1/4 cup butter or margarine, melted and cooled

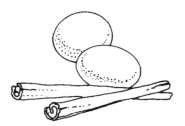

Beat egg white in a small bowl until stiff and set aside. Mix together dry ingredients and set aside. Combine egg yolk, eggnog and butter. Add to dry ingredients, mixing until just blended. Fold in beaten egg white until just mixed. Do not over-beat batter.

SWEET CREAM WAFFLES

Serve this rich waffle with any of the delectable toppings found on pages 133 to 142.

2 eggs, room temperature and separated
1 cup all-purpose flour
1 tsp. baking powder
2 tbs. sugar
1/8 tsp. salt
3/4 cup heavy cream (whipping cream)
1/4 cup butter or margarine, melted and cooled

Beat egg white in a small bowl until stiff and set aside. Mix together dry ingredients and set aside. Combine egg yolks, cream and butter. Add to dry ingredients, mixing until just blended. Fold in beaten egg whites until just mixed. Do not overbeat batter.

Variation: LEMON CREAM WAFFLES
Add lemon peel and lemon juice. Use 3/4 cup cream and 2 eggs instead of 1.

20   WHITE FLOUR, CHEESE AND MEAT WAFFLES

MAPLE WAFFLES

Enjoy the maple syrup baked right into the waffles!

1 egg, room temperature and separated
1 1/4 cups all-purpose flour
1 tsp. baking powder
1/8 tsp. salt
3/4 cup milk
2 tbs. maple syrup
3 tbs. butter or margarine, melted and cooled

Beat egg white in a small bowl until stiff and set aside. Mix together dry ingredients and set aside. Combine egg yolk, milk, syrup and melted butter. Add to dry ingredients, mixing until just blended. Fold in beaten egg white until just mixed. Do not overbeat batter.

COCONUT CHOCOLATE CHIP WAFFLES

Serve this well-loved combination with chocolate or maple syrup. These waffles can be enjoyed for either a rich breakfast or dessert.

1 egg, room temperature and
   separated
1 cup all-purpose flour
1 tsp. baking powder
1/8 tsp. salt

1/3 cup coconut flakes
3/4 cup canned coconut cream
1/4 cup butter or margarine, melted and
   cooled
1/3 cup chocolate chips

Beat egg white in a small bowl until stiff and set aside. Mix together dry ingredients and set aside. Combine egg yolk, coconut cream and butter. Add to dry ingredients, mixing until just blended. Add chocolate chips and fold in with beaten egg white until just mixed. Do not overbeat batter.

Variation: BUTTERSCOTCH WAFFLES

Use canned evaporated milk instead of the coconut cream; use butterscotch chips instead of chocolate chips.

WHITE CHOCOLATE WAFFLES

Here's another waffle you won't be able to resist. The vanilla and white chocolate combination is superb.

1 egg, room temperature and separated
1 cup all-purpose flour
1 tsp. baking powder
1/8 tsp. salt
1 tbs. sugar
2/3 cup milk
2 tsp. vanilla extract
1/4 cup butter or margarine, melted and cooled
1/3 cup white chocolate or vanilla chips

Beat egg white in a small bowl until stiff and set aside. Mix together dry ingredients and set aside. Combine egg yolk, milk, vanilla and butter. Add to dry ingredients, mixing until just blended. Add white chocolate chips or vanilla chips and fold in with egg white until just mixed. Do not overbeat batter.

COTTAGE CHEESE WAFFLES

This rises nicely to make a fluffy waffle, rich in taste. It's best if cooked longer than normal so it's a little crispier.

1 egg, room temperature and separated
1 cup all-purpose flour
1 tsp. baking powder
$1/8$ tsp. salt
1 tbs. sugar

$1/8$ tsp. baking soda
$3/4$ cup milk
$1/2$ cup cottage cheese
$1/4$ cup butter or margarine, melted and cooled

Beat egg white in a small bowl until stiff and set aside. Mix together dry ingredients and set aside. Combine egg yolk, milk, cottage cheese and melted butter. Add to dry ingredients, mixing until just blended. Fold in beaten egg white until just mixed. Do not overbeat batter.

Variation: YOGURT or RICOTTA WAFFLES
Use yogurt or ricotta cheese in place of the cottage cheese.

SOUR CREAM WAFFLES

An incredibly light and tender waffle. Not meant for counting calories!

4 eggs, room temperature and separated
1 cup all-purpose flour
1 tsp. baking powder
$1/8$ tsp. salt
$1/3$ cup sugar
1 cup sour cream
$1/4$ cup butter or margarine, melted and cooled

Beat egg whites in a small bowl until stiff and set aside. Mix together dry ingredients and set aside. Combine egg yolks, sour cream and melted butter. Add to dry ingredients, mixing until just blended. Fold in beaten egg whites until just mixed. Do not over-beat batter.

POTATO WAFFLES

You will find a delicate taste of potato in this fluffy waffle.

1 egg, room temperature and separated
1 cup all-purpose flour
1 tsp. baking powder
$1/8$ tsp. salt
1 tbs. sugar
$1/2$ cup mashed potatoes
$3/4$ cup potato or regular water
$1/4$ cup butter or margarine, melted and cooled

Beat egg white in a small bowl until stiff and set aside.
Mix together dry ingredients and set aside. Combine egg yolk, potatoes,
water and melted butter. Add to dry ingredients, mixing until just blended. Fold in
beaten egg white until just mixed. Do not overbeat batter.

BACON WAFFLES

This is a true winner. For added bacon flavor, cut a slice of uncooked bacon into two or three pieces and place on top of the batter prior to heating. Heat a minute or two longer than normal, allowing the bacon to cook. You'll be coming back for more of these.

1 egg, room temperature and separated
1 1/4 cups all-purpose flour
1 tsp. baking powder
1/8 tsp. salt

1 tbs. brown sugar
3/4 cup milk
1/4 cup butter, melted and cooled
1/2 cup cooked, crumbled bacon

Beat egg white in a small bowl until stiff and set aside. Mix together dry ingredients and set aside. Combine egg yolk, milk and butter. Add to dry ingredients, mixing until just blended. Add bacon and fold in with beaten egg white until just mixed. Do not overbeat batter.

Variation: CHEDDAR CHEESE AND BACON WAFFLES
Add 1/2 cup grated cheddar cheese when you add the bacon.

Variation: CHEDDAR CHEESE WAFFLES
Substitute grated cheddar cheese for the bacon.

MEAT WAFFLES

Use leftovers for these waffles, which make a great lunch or supper, served with soup and/or salad. Or, serve with a slice of tomato and Welsh Rarebit.

1 egg, room temperature and separated
1 1/4 cups all-purpose or whole wheat flour
1 tsp. baking powder
1/8 tsp. salt
1 tsp. sugar

3/4 cup milk
2 tbs. butter or margarine, melted and cooled
1/2 cup cooked, diced ham, turkey or chicken

Beat egg white in a small bowl until stiff and set aside. Mix together dry ingredients and set aside. Combine egg yolk, milk and butter. Add to dry ingredients, mixing until just blended. Add meat and fold in with beaten egg white until just mixed. Do not overbeat batter.

Variation: ITALIAN or COUNTRY SAUSAGE WAFFLES

Use 1/2 cup cooked, diced Italian or country sausage and 1 tsp. dried basil or oregano, or 1 tbs. chopped fresh.

WESTERN WAFFLES

This is an outstanding brunch or light lunch waffle. Serve it with a salsa if desired.

1 egg, room temperature and
   separated
1 cup all-purpose flour
1 tsp. baking powder
1/8 tsp. salt
1/2 tsp. sugar
3/4 cup milk

1/4 cup grated cheddar cheese
1–1 1/2 tbs. finely diced red onion
3 tbs. finely diced green bell pepper
1/4 cup cooked, crumbled bacon
1/4 cup butter or margarine, melted and
   cooled

Beat egg white in a small bowl until stiff and set aside. Mix together dry ingredients and set aside. Combine egg yolk, milk, cheese, onion, pepper, bacon and butter. Add to dry ingredients, mixing until just blended. Fold in beaten egg white until just mixed. Do not over-beat batter.

MEXICAN WAFFLES

For a real change-of-pace dinner, serve these waffles with melted cheese and jalapeños.

1 egg, room temperature and
   separated
1/2 cup all-purpose flour
1/2 cup cornmeal
1 tsp. baking powder
1/8 tsp. salt
1 tsp. sugar

2/3 cup milk
1/4 cup salsa
1/2 cup ground meat cooked with taco
   seasoning*
1/4 cup butter or margarine, melted and
   cooled

Beat egg white in a small bowl until stiff and set aside. Mix together dry ingredients and set aside. Combine egg yolk, milk, salsa, meat and butter. Add to dry ingredients, mixing until just blended. Fold in beaten egg white until just mixed. Do not overbeat batter.

*The envelope of taco seasoning is normally used with 1 lb. of ground meat. For convenience, I cook the whole amount and freeze portions for later use.

GREEK CHEESE AND SPINACH WAFFLES

Serve these unique waffles for lunch or a light dinner with a Greek salad.

1 egg, room temperature and
  separated
1 cup all-purpose flour
1 tsp. baking powder
1/8 tsp. salt
1/2 tsp. sugar
dash garlic powder

1/4 tsp. dried dill, optional
3/4 cup milk
1/3 cup crumbled feta cheese
1/3 cup cooked, drained, chopped
  spinach
1/4 cup olive oil, or butter or margarine,
  melted

Beat egg white in a small bowl until stiff and set aside. Mix together dry ingredients and set aside. Combine egg yolk, milk, cheese, spinach and oil. Add to dry ingredients, mixing until just blended. Fold in beaten egg white until just mixed. Do not overbeat batter.

WHOLE GRAIN, CEREAL AND SPICE WAFFLES

WHOLE WHEAT WAFFLES

In addition to breakfast, this is a great waffle for lunch or supper. Serve with soup and a salad.

1 egg, room temperature and separated
3/4 cup whole wheat flour
1/4 cup wheat bran
2 tbs. wheat germ
1 tsp. baking powder
1/8 tsp. salt
3/4 cup milk
1 tbs. honey
2 tbs. butter, melted and cooled

Beat egg white in a small bowl until stiff and set aside. Mix together dry ingredients and set aside. Combine egg yolk, milk, honey and melted butter. Add to dry ingredients, mixing until just blended. Fold in beaten egg white until just mixed. Do not overbeat batter.

HEALTHY WHOLE GRAIN WAFFLES

Use these waffles as a base for a delightful sandwich or meal.

1 egg, room temperature and separated
$1/2$ cup whole wheat flour
$1/3$ cup oats
$1/4$ cup oat bran
2 tbs. wheat germ
1 tsp. baking powder
$1/8$ tsp. salt
$3/4$ cup milk or water
1 tbs. honey
2 tbs. butter or margarine, melted and cooled

Beat egg white in a small bowl until stiff and set aside. Mix together dry ingredients and set aside. Combine egg yolk, milk or water, honey and butter. Add to dry ingredients, mixing until just blended. Fold in beaten egg white until just mixed. Do not overbeat batter.

SEVEN OR NINE GRAIN WAFFLES

3–4 waffles

This recipe makes a medium-to-thick batter which rises nicely, and produces a crunchy, flavorful whole grain waffle.

1 egg, room temperature and separated
1 cup whole wheat flour or all-purpose flour
$\frac{1}{2}$ cup 7 or 9 grain cereal
1 tsp. baking powder

$\frac{1}{8}$ tsp. salt
$\frac{3}{4}$ cup milk
2 tbs. honey
$\frac{1}{4}$ cup butter or margarine, melted and cooled

Beat egg white in a small bowl until stiff and set aside. Mix together dry ingredients and set aside. Combine egg yolk, milk, honey and melted butter. Add to dry ingredients, mixing until just blended. Fold in beaten egg white until just mixed. Do not overbeat batter.

Note: 7 or 9 grain cereal is available in health food stores, by mail order, or some larger grocery stores.

Variation: GRANOLA WAFFLES

Substitute $\frac{3}{4}$ cup granola cereal for the 7 or 9 grain cereal.

WHEAT FLAKE WAFFLES

Wheat flakes are similar in processing to oats. The flakes have a delicious, nutty flavor. In addition they retain much of the nutritional value of the wheat berry which is lost in the refining of the kernel to flour. Bake longer for a crispier waffle.

1 egg, room temperature and separated
3/4 cup whole wheat flour
3/4 cup wheat flakes
1 tsp. baking powder
1/8 tsp. salt
3/4 cup milk
1 tbs. honey
1/4 cup butter, melted and cooled

Beat egg white in a small bowl until stiff and set aside. Mix together dry ingredients and set aside. Combine egg yolk, milk, honey and melted butter. Add to dry ingredients, mixing until just blended. Fold in beaten egg white until just mixed. Do not overbeat batter.

OATMEAL WAFFLES

Here's a must for oatmeal lovers. This is an extremely moist, incredibly good waffle. It's better if cooked a little longer than normal for some crispiness.

1 egg, room temperature and separated
1 1/2 cups oats
1 tsp. baking powder
1/8 tsp. salt
1 tbs. brown sugar
3/4 cup milk
1/4 cup butter or margarine, melted and cooled

Beat egg white in a small bowl until stiff and set aside. Mix together dry ingredients and set aside. Combine egg yolk, milk and melted butter. Add to dry ingredients, mixing until just blended. Fold in beaten egg white until just mixed. Do not overbeat batter.

CORN WAFFLES

For Southwestern flavor, top with with chili or salsa. For a Southern treat, serve with a creamed chicken topping.

1 egg, room temperature and separated
1/2 cup all-purpose flour
1/2 cup cornmeal
1 tsp. baking powder
1/8 tsp. salt
3/4 cup milk
1/2 cup corn kernels
1 tbs. honey
1/4 cup butter or margarine, melted and cooled

Beat egg white in a small bowl until stiff and set aside.
Mix together dry ingredients and set aside. Combine egg yolk, milk, corn, honey and butter. Add to dry ingredients, mixing until just blended. Fold in beaten egg white until just mixed. Do not overbeat batter.

OAT BRAN WAFFLES

These are tasty and so nutritional too!

1 egg, room temperature and separated
½ cup all-purpose flour
½ cup oats, quick cooking or regular
½ cup oat bran (wheat or rice bran can also be used)
1 tsp. baking powder
⅛ tsp. salt
¾ cup milk
1 tbs. honey
¼ cup butter or margarine, melted and cooled

Beat egg white in a small bowl until stiff and set aside. Mix together dry ingredients and set aside. Combine egg yolk, milk, honey and butter. Add to dry ingredients, mixing until just blended. Fold in beaten egg white until just mixed. Do not overbeat batter.

BUCKWHEAT WAFFLES

Buckwheat is a strong-tasting flour, which is why such a small amount is used. One of the most common uses of the flour is for pancakes and waffles.

1 egg, room temperature and separated
1 cup all-purpose flour
1/4 cup buckwheat flour
1 tsp. baking powder
1/8 tsp. salt
3/4 cup milk
1 tbs. honey
1/4 cup butter or margarine, melted and cooled

Beat egg white in a small bowl until stiff and set aside. Mix together dry ingredients and set aside. Combine egg yolk, milk, honey and butter. Add to dry ingredients, mixing until just blended. Fold in beaten egg white until just mixed. Do not overbeat batter.

Note: Try using any of these flours which have high nutritional contents: quinoa, amaranth, teff, flaxseed.

BANANA BRAN WAFFLES

This flavorful waffle has the nutritional benefits of bran.

1 egg, room temperature and separated
1/2 cup all-purpose flour
1/4 cup oats, quick cooking or regular
1/4 cup oat, wheat or rice bran
1 tsp. baking powder
1/8 tsp. salt
1 tbs. brown sugar
1/2 cup milk
1 medium banana, mashed
1/4 cup butter or margarine melted and cooled
2–3 tbs. chopped nuts, optional

Beat egg white in a small bowl until stiff and set aside. Mix together dry ingredients and set aside. Combine egg yolk, milk, banana and butter. Add to dry ingredients, mixing until just blended. Add nuts and fold in with beaten egg white until just mixed. Do not overbeat batter.

RICE WAFFLES

If you like the taste and texture of rice, you'll enjoy this light waffle.

1 egg, room temperature and separated
1 cup all-purpose flour
3/4 cup cooked rice
1 tsp. baking powder
1/8 tsp. salt

1 tbs. white or brown sugar
3/4 cup milk
1/4 cup butter or margarine, melted and
    cooled

Beat egg white in a small bowl until stiff and set aside. Mix together dry ingredients and set aside. Combine egg yolk, milk and butter. Add to dry ingredients, mixing until just blended. Fold in rice and beaten egg white until just mixed. Do not overbeat batter.

Variation: COCONUT RICE WAFFLES
Substitute canned coconut cream for the regular milk and add 2 tbs. coconut flakes.

Variation: WILD RICE WAFFLES
Use 1 1/4 cups all-purpose flour and 1/2 cup cooked wild rice.

RYE WAFFLES

The taste is a real surprise unless you know it's coming! A must for rye lovers.

1 egg, room temperature and separated
1/2 cup all-purpose flour
1/2 cup rye flour
1 tsp. baking powder
1/8 tsp. salt

1 tsp. caraway seeds, or to taste
3/4 cup milk
1 tbs. honey
1/4 cup butter or margarine, melted and
   cooled

Beat egg white in a small bowl until stiff and set aside. Mix together dry ingredients and set aside. Combine egg yolk, milk, honey and butter. Add to dry ingredients, mixing until just blended. Fold in beaten egg white until just mixed. Do not overbeat batter.

Variation: SCANDANAVIAN RYE WAFFLES
Reduce the amount of caraway seeds to 1/2 tsp.; add 1/4 tsp. orange peel and 1/2 tsp. fennel seed. Substitute molasses for the honey.

SPICE WAFFLES

Here's a great change-of-pace waffle, perfect for a cold, raining, lazy day. Serve with apple butter, Sautéed Apples, page 137, or applesauce (warm in microwave if desired).

1 egg, room temperature and separated	$1/8$ tsp. ground cloves
1 cup all-purpose flour	$1/2$ tsp. cinnamon
1 tsp. baking powder	$1/16$ tsp. nutmeg
$1/8$ tsp. salt	$3/4$ cup milk
1 tbs. brown sugar	$1/4$ cup butter or margarine, melted and cooled

Beat egg white in a small bowl until stiff and set aside. Mix together dry ingredients and set aside. Combine egg yolk, milk and butter. Add to dry ingredients, mixing until just blended. Fold in beaten egg white until just mixed. Do not overbeat batter.

Variation: SPICED APPLE WAFFLES

Add $1/4$ medium apple, peeled and diced, and 2 to 3 tbs. chopped walnuts. Fold both in with the egg white.

SAFFRON WAFFLES

Saffron is one of the world's most expensive spices, but only the smallest amount is used to achieve the wonderful color and taste in these waffles.

1 egg, room temperature and separated
1 cup all-purpose flour
1 tsp. baking powder
1/8 tsp. salt
1 tbs. sugar
1/8 tsp. saffron threads, or 1/16 tsp. powdered saffron
1/8 tsp. nutmeg
3/4 cup milk
1/4 cup butter or margarine, melted and cooled
2–3 tbs. raisins, optional

Beat egg white in a small bowl until stiff and set aside. Mix together dry ingredients and set aside. Combine egg yolk, milk and butter. Add to dry ingredients, mixing until just blended. Add raisins if desired and fold in with beaten egg white until just mixed. Do not overbeat batter.

POPPY SEED WAFFLES

Poppy seeds give a sweet, delicate taste to this waffle.

1 egg, room temperature and separated
1 cup all-purpose flour
1 tsp. baking powder
1/8 tsp. salt
1 tbs. sugar

2 tsp.–1 tbs. poppy seeds, or to taste
3/4 cup milk
1 tsp. almond extract
1/4 cup butter or margarine, melted
   and cooled

Beat egg white in a small bowl until stiff and set aside. Mix together dry ingredients and set aside. Combine egg yolk, milk, almond extract and melted butter. Add to dry ingredients, mixing until just blended. Fold in beaten egg white until just mixed. Do not overbeat batter.

Variation: ANISE WAFFLES
Delete almond extract and poppy seeds. Add 1 tsp. each anise and sesame seeds.

Variation: CARAWAY WAFFLES
Delete almond extract and poppy seeds. Substitute honey for sugar and add 1 1/2 to 2 tsp. caraway seeds.

VANILLA WAFFLES

This recipe makes a light batter and waffle with wonderful vanilla flavor. For best results, use real vanilla instead of imitation.

1 egg, room temperature and separated
1 cup all-purpose flour
1 tsp. baking powder
1/8 tsp. salt
1 tbs. brown sugar
3/4 cup milk
1 tbs. vanilla extract
3 tbs. butter or margarine, melted and cooled

Beat egg white in a small bowl until stiff and set aside. Mix together dry ingredients and set aside. Combine egg yolk, milk, vanilla and butter. Add to dry ingredients, mixing until just blended. Fold in beaten egg white until just mixed. Do not overbeat batter.

CRYSTALLIZED GINGER WAFFLES

Wow! You're going to love this! Crystallized ginger is pieces of ginger root which have been candied and sugared. Jars or boxes of crystallized or candied ginger may be found in a well-stocked spice section of your grocery, wherever Chinese groceries are sold, in gourmet shops or by mail order. When the ginger is chopped with your food processor or blender   it becomes soft and pliable.

1 egg, room temperature and
  separated
1 1/4 cups all-purpose flour
1 tsp. baking powder
1 tbs. brown sugar
3/4 cup milk
1 tbs. pure vanilla extract

1 tsp. chopped crystallized ginger, or
  to taste
1/4 cup butter or margarine, melted
  and cooled
1/4 cup chopped nuts (walnuts, pecans
  or macadamias)
1/4 cup chocolate chips

Beat egg white in a small bowl until stiff and set aside. Mix together dry ingredients and set aside. Combine egg yolk, milk, vanilla, ginger and butter. Add to dry ingredients, mixing until just blended. Add nuts and chocolate chips; fold in with beaten egg white until just mixed. Do not overbeat batter.

CARDAMOM WAFFLES

Cardamom has a very distinctive taste and is commonly used in Scandinavian sweets and breads. Look for it in well-stocked grocery stores or gourmet shops.

1 egg, room temperature and separated
1 1/4 cups all-purpose flour
1 tsp. baking powder
1/8 tsp. salt
1/8 tsp. orange peel
1/8 tsp. lemon peel
1/4 tsp. ground cardamom
3/4 cup milk
1 tbs. honey
1/4 cup butter or margarine, melted and cooled

Beat egg white in a small bowl until stiff and set aside. Mix together dry ingredients and set aside. Combine egg yolk, milk, honey and butter. Add to dry ingredients, mixing until just blended. Fold in beaten egg white until just mixed. Do not overbeat batter.

FRUIT WAFFLES

52	Apple Waffles
53	Banana Waffles
54	Strawberry Waffles
55	Hawaiian Waffles
56	Cranberry Pineapple Waffles
57	Coconut Pineapple Waffles
58	Orange Banana Waffles
59	Strawberry Banana Waffles
60	Peach Waffles
60	Apple or Pear Waffles
61	Banana, Coconut and Macadamia Waffles
62	Orange Cinnamon Oatmeal Waffles
63	Cranberry Waffles
64	Cran-Orange Waffles
65	Apple Cider Waffles
66	Apple Oatmeal Waffles

67	Apple Carrot Waffles
68	Carrot, Cherry and Coconut Waffles
69	Pineapple Strawberry Waffles
70	Grape Apple Waffles
71	Grape Orange Waffles
72	Citrus Pineapple Waffles
73	Pineapple Papaya Waffles
74	Cranapple Waffles
75	Banana Pineapple Waffles
76	Orange Apple Waffles
77	Pineapple, Strawberry and Banana Waffles
78	Pineapple Orange Mint Waffles
79	West Indian Banana Waffles
80	Pumpkin Waffles
81	Cinnamon Raisin Waffles

Note: See Nut and Nut Butter Waffles, *page 82, for additional waffles which include fruits.*

APPLE WAFFLES

A delicate taste of apples gives these waffles a special flavor.

1 egg, room temperature and separated
1 cup all-purpose flour
1 tsp. baking powder
$1/8$ tsp. salt
$1/8$ tsp. cinnamon
1 tbs. sugar
$2/3$ cup apple juice
$1/4$ cup butter or margarine, melted and cooled
$1/4$ medium apple, peeled and diced

Beat egg white in a small bowl until stiff and set aside. Mix together dry ingredients and set aside. Combine egg yolk, juice and melted butter. Add to dry ingredients, mixing until just blended. Add diced apple and fold in with beaten egg white until just mixed. Do not overbeat batter.

BANANA WAFFLES

This superb banana waffle has lots of that favorite banana flavor. Very moist.

1 egg, room temperature and separated
1 cup all-purpose flour
1 tsp. baking powder
$1/8$ tsp. salt
1 tbs. sugar
$1/2$ cup milk
1 cup mashed banana (about 2 medium, well-ripened bananas)
$1/4$ cup butter or margarine, melted and cooled
2–3 tbs. chopped nuts (walnuts or pecans)

Beat egg white in a small bowl until stiff and set aside. Mix together dry ingredients and set aside. Combine egg yolk, milk, banana and melted butter. Add to dry ingredients, mixing until just blended. Add nuts and fold in with beaten egg white until just mixed. Do not overbeat batter.

STRABERRY WAFFLES

3 waffles

Who doesn't love hot waffles served with a favorite berry? Bake the berry into the waffle itself for a truly wonderful breakfast treat. Serve them as a dessert with ice cream. Raspberries, blackberries, blueberries or other berries can also be used.

1 egg, room temperature and separated
1 cup all-purpose flour
1 tsp. baking powder
1/8 tsp. salt
1/3 cup milk
1 tbs. honey or strawberry (or other berry) syrup

1/2 cup pureed strawberries, fresh or thawed frozen
3 tbs. butter or margarine, melted and cooled
1/4–1/3 cup chopped nuts, optional

Beat egg white in a small bowl until stiff and set aside. Mix together dry ingredients and set aside. Combine egg yolk, milk, honey or syrup, strawberries and melted butter. Add to dry ingredients, mixing until just blended. Add nuts, if desired, and fold in with beaten egg white until just mixed. Do not overbeat batter.

HAWAIIAN WAFFLES

This is a treat for breakfast or dessert.

1 egg, room temperature and separated
3/4 cup all-purpose flour
1/2 cup oatmeal
1 tsp. baking powder
1/8 tsp. salt
1 tbs. brown sugar
2 tbs. coconut flakes
3/4 cup Mauna Lai (or similar juice), or milk
1/4 cup butter, melted and cooled to warm
1–2 tbs. chocolate chips
1–2 tbs. chopped macadamia nuts

Beat egg white in a small bowl until stiff and set aside. Mix together dry ingredients and set aside. Combine egg yolk, juice or milk and melted butter. Add to dry ingredients, mixing until just blended. Add chocolate chips and nuts. Fold in with beaten egg white until just mixed. Do not overbeat batter.

CRANBERRY PINEAPPLE WAFFLES

Here is a delightful treat for Thanksgiving or any fall morning.

1 egg, room temperature and separated
1 cup all-purpose flour
1 tsp. baking powder
1/8 tsp. salt
1 tbs. brown sugar
2/3 cup pineapple or cranberry juice
1/4 cup crushed pineapple, drained
1/4 cup chopped cranberries
1/4 cup butter, melted and cooled
2–3 tbs. chopped pecans or walnuts, optional

Beat egg white in a small bowl until stiff and set aside. Mix together dry ingredients and set aside. Combine egg yolk, juice, pineapple, cranberries and melted butter. Add to dry ingredients, mixing until just blended. Add nuts, if desired, and fold in with beaten egg white until just mixed. Do not overbeat batter.

COCONUT PINEAPPLE WAFFLES

Try this delightful tropical waffle.

1 egg, room temperature and separated
1 cup all-purpose flour
1 tsp. baking powder
1/8 tsp. salt
1 tbs. brown sugar
2 tbs. coconut flakes
1/2 cup pineapple juice
1/4 cup crushed pineapple, well drained
1/4 cup butter or margarine, melted and cooled

Beat egg white in a small bowl until stiff and set aside. Mix together dry ingredients and set aside. Combine egg yolk, juice, pineapple and melted butter. Add to dry ingredients, mixing until just blended. Fold in beaten egg white until just mixed. Do not overbeat batter.

ORANGE BANANA WAFFLES

This favorite combination is sure to be a winner.

1 egg, room temperature and separated
1 cup all-purpose flour
1 tsp. baking powder
$1/8$ tsp. salt
1 tbs. sugar
$1/2$ cup orange juice
$1/3$ cup mashed banana
$1/4$ cup butter or margarine, melted and
   cooled

Beat egg white in a small bowl until stiff
and set aside. Mix together dry ingredients and
set aside. Combine egg yolk, juice, banana and melted butter. Add to dry ingredients, mixing until just blended. Fold in beaten egg white until just mixed. Do not overbeat batter.

STRAWBERRY BANANA WAFFLES

3 waffles

What a pleasing combination! The batter is somewhat thicker than normal.

1 egg, room temperature and separated
1 tsp. baking powder
1 cup all-purpose flour
$1/8$ tsp. salt
$1/4$ cup milk
1 tbs. strawberry syrup or honey
$1/4$ cup pureed strawberries
$1/4$ cup mashed bananas
$1/4$ cup butter or margarine, melted and cooled

Beat egg white in a small bowl until stiff and set aside. Mix together dry ingredients and set aside. Combine egg yolk, milk, syrup or honey, strawberries, banana and melted butter. Add to dry ingredients, mixing until just blended. Fold in beaten egg white until just mixed. Do not overbeat batter.

FRUIT WAFFLES   59

PEACH WAFFLES

You'll enjoy the delicate peach flavoring. Serve with Peach and Orange Syrup, *page 141, for a tasty delight.*

1 egg, room temperature and separated
1 cup all-purpose flour
1 tsp. baking powder
1/8 tsp. salt
2 tsp. brown sugar

1/8 tsp. cinnamon
1 cup peach puree
1/4 cup butter or margarine, melted
    and cooled

Beat egg white in a small bowl until stiff and set aside. Mix together dry ingredients and set aside. Combine egg yolk, peach puree and melted butter. Add to dry ingredients, mixing until just blended. Fold in beaten egg white until just mixed. Do not overbeat batter.

Note: Puree peeled fresh or rinsed canned peaches in a food processor.

Variation: APPLE or PEAR WAFFLES

Substitute apple or pear puree for the peach puree. Fresh apples or pears should be cooked in almost boiling water until soft prior to pureeing.

BANANA, COCONUT AND MACADAMIA WAFFLES 3 waffles

Three different tastes blend into one out-of-this-world waffle.

1 egg, room temperature and separated
1 cup all-purpose flour
1 tsp. baking powder
1/8 tsp. salt
1 tsp. brown sugar
2 tbs. coconut flakes
1/2 cup canned coconut milk or regular milk
1/2 cup mashed banana
1 tsp. coconut extract or vanilla extract
1/4 cup butter or margarine, melted and cooled
1/4–1/3 cup chopped macadamias, or walnuts

Beat egg white in a small bowl until stiff and set aside. Mix together dry ingredients and set aside. Combine egg yolk, coconut milk, banana, coconut extract and melted butter. Add to dry ingredients, mixing until just blended. Add nuts and fold in with beaten egg white until just mixed. Do not overbeat batter.

ORANGE CINNAMON OATMEAL WAFFLES

This delicious oatmeal waffle has a great orange flavor.

1 egg, room temperature and separated
$1/2$ cup all-purpose flour
1 cup oats
1 tsp. baking powder
$1/8$ tsp. salt
1 tbs. brown sugar
$1/2$ tsp. cinnamon
$1/8$ tsp. orange peel
$3/4$ cup orange juice
$1/4$ cup butter or margarine, melted and cooled
$1/4$ cup chopped walnuts, optional

Beat egg white in a small bowl until stiff and set aside. Mix together dry ingredients and set aside. Combine egg yolk, juice and butter. Add to dry ingredients, mixing until just blended. Add nuts, if desired, and fold in with beaten egg white until just mixed. Do not overbeat batter.

CRANBERRY WAFFLES

This tangy waffle is great served with Cranberry Butter, *page 135.*

1 egg, room temperature and separated
1 cup all-purpose flour
1 tsp. baking powder
$\frac{1}{8}$ tsp. salt
$\frac{3}{4}$ cup cranberry juice
2–3 tbs. chopped fresh cranberries, or to taste
1 tbs. honey
3 tbs. butter or margarine, melted and cooled

Beat egg white in a small bowl until stiff and set aside. Mix together dry ingredients and set aside. Combine egg yolk, juice, cranberries, honey and butter. Add to dry ingredients, mixing until just blended. Fold in beaten egg white until just mixed. Do not overbeat batter.

CRAN-ORANGE WAFFLES

The dried cranberries, which add lots of zest to these waffles, may be found in some large grocery stores, gourmet shops or by mail order. Use in place of raisins in any of your favorite recipes for a change-of-pace treat.

1 egg, room temperature and separated
1 cup all-purpose flour
1 tsp. baking powder
1/8 tsp. salt
1 tbs. brown sugar
1 tsp. orange peel

1/4 cup milk
1/2 cup orange juice
1/4 cup butter or margarine, melted
  and cooled
1/4–1/3 cup dried cranberries

Beat egg white in a small bowl until stiff and set aside. Mix together dry ingredients and set aside. Combine egg yolk, milk, juice and butter. Add to dry ingredients, mixing until just blended. Add cranberries and fold in with beaten egg white until just mixed. Do not overbeat batter.

APPLE CIDER WAFFLES

The orange peel is the secret ingredient which makes these waffles surprise you with an unexpected taste.

1 egg, room temperature and separated
1 cup all-purpose flour
1 tsp. baking powder
$\frac{1}{8}$ tsp. salt
1 tbs. brown sugar
$\frac{1}{4}$ tsp. orange peel
$\frac{2}{3}$ cup apple cider, or apple juice
$\frac{1}{4}$ medium apple, peeled and diced
$\frac{1}{4}$ cup butter or margarine, melted and cooled

Beat egg white in a small bowl until stiff and set aside. Mix together dry ingredients and set aside. Combine egg yolk, cider, apple and butter. Add to dry ingredients, mixing until just blended. Fold in beaten egg white until just mixed. Do not overbeat batter.

APPLE OATMEAL WAFFLES

Favorite ingredients make one of the best waffles. Do not overcook.

1 egg, room temperature and
  separated
3/4 cup all-purpose flour
3/4 cup oats
1 tsp. baking powder
1/8 tsp. salt
1/2 tsp. cinnamon
3/4 cup apple juice

1 tbs. honey
1/4 cup butter or margarine, melted
  and cooled
1/4 medium apple, peeled and diced,
  or 1–2 tbs. diced dried apples
1/4 cup chopped walnuts, optional
2 tbs. raisins, optional

Beat egg white in a small bowl until stiff and set aside. Mix together dry ingredients and set aside. Combine egg yolk, juice, honey and butter. Add to dry ingredients, mixing until just blended. Add apple, nuts and raisins; fold in with beaten egg white until just mixed. Do not overbeat batter.

APPLE CARROT WAFFLES

Apples and carrots make a surprisingly tasty combination.

1 egg, room temperature and separated
1 cup all-purpose flour
1 tsp. baking powder
1/8 tsp. salt
1/8 tsp. cinnamon
1 tbs. brown sugar
2/3 cup apple juice

1/4 cup grated carrots
1/4 apple, peeled and finely diced
1/4 cup butter or margarine, melted
    and cooled
2–3 tbs. raisins, optional
2–3 tbs. chopped walnuts, optional

Beat egg white in a small bowl until stiff and set aside. Mix together dry ingredients and set aside. Combine egg yolk, juice, carrots, apple and butter. Add to dry ingredients, mixing until just blended. Add raisins and nuts, if desired, and fold in with beaten egg white until just mixed. Do not overbeat batter.

CARROT, CHERRY AND COCONUT WAFFLES

3 waffles

A cake-like waffle, this doesn't even need syrup. (Of course syrup may ALWAYS be used.)

1 egg, room temperature and separated
1 cup all-purpose flour
1 tsp. baking powder
1/8 tsp. salt
1 tsp. sugar
1/8 tsp. cinnamon
1 tbs. flaked coconut

3/4 cup canned coconut milk
1/4 cup grated carrots
6 maraschino cherries, halved or quartered
1/4 cup butter or margarine, melted and cooled
1/4–1/3 cup chopped walnuts

Beat egg white in a small bowl until stiff and set aside. Mix together dry ingredients and set aside. Combine egg yolk, coconut milk, carrots, cherries and butter. Add to dry ingredients, mixing until just blended. Add nuts and fold in with beaten egg white until just mixed. Do not overbeat batter.

PINEAPPLE STRAWBERRY WAFFLES

This fruity waffle is moist and unique.

1 egg, room temperature and separated
1 cup all-purpose flour
1 tsp. baking powder
1/8 tsp. salt
1 tbs. sugar
1/2 cup strawberries, pureed
1/4 cup pineapple juice
1/4 cup crushed pineapple, drained
1/4 cup butter or margarine, melted and cooled

Beat egg white in a small bowl until stiff and set aside. Mix together dry ingredients and set aside. Combine egg yolk, strawberries, juice, pineapple and butter. Add to dry ingredients, mixing until just blended. Fold in beaten egg white until just mixed. Do not overbeat batter.

GRAPE APPLE WAFFLES

This recipe makes a delicate, flavorful waffle.

1 egg, room temperature and separated
1 1/4 cups all-purpose flour
1 tsp. baking powder
1/8 tsp. salt
1 tbs. sugar
1/2 tsp. lemon peel
3/4 cup white grape juice
1/4 cup butter or margarine, melted and cooled
1/4 medium apple, peeled and diced, or pear

Beat egg white in a small bowl until stiff and set aside. Mix together dry ingredients and set aside. Combine egg yolk, juice, apple and butter. Add to dry ingredients, mixing until just blended. Fold in beaten egg white until just mixed. Do not overbeat batter.

GRAPE ORANGE WAFFLES

Here's a wonderful combination.

1 egg, room temperature and separated
1 cup all-purpose flour
1 tsp. baking powder
$\frac{1}{8}$ tsp. salt
1 tbs. sugar

$\frac{1}{2}$ cup white grape juice
$\frac{1}{2}$ cup Mandarin orange segments
$\frac{1}{4}$ cup butter or margarine, melted
    and cooled
$\frac{1}{4}$ tsp. orange peel

Beat egg white in a small bowl until stiff and set aside. Mix together dry ingredients and set aside. Combine egg yolk, juice, orange segments and butter. Add to dry ingredients, mixing until just blended. Fold in orange peel and beaten egg white until just mixed. Do not over-beat batter.

Note: The Mandarin orange segments will become somewhat crushed during the mixing, which adds liquid to the batter, but you will also have orange chunks in the waffles, adding a nice texture.

CITRUS PINEAPPLE WAFFLES

This moist waffle has lots of fruity flavor.

1 egg, room temperature and separated
1 cup all-purpose flour
1 tsp. baking powder
$1/8$ tsp. salt
1 tbs. sugar
$1/4$ tsp. orange peel
$1/3$ cup grapefruit juice
$1/3$ cup orange juice
$1/4$ cup crushed pineapple, drained
$1/4$ cup butter or margarine, melted and cooled

Beat egg white in a small bowl until stiff and set aside. Mix together dry ingredients and set aside. Combine egg yolk, juices, pineapple and butter. Add to dry ingredients, mixing until just blended. Fold in beaten egg white until just mixed. Do not overbeat batter.

PINEAPPLE PAPAYA WAFFLES

What a combination! You'll love it.

1 egg, room temperature and separated
1 cup all-purpose flour
1 tsp. baking powder
1/8 tsp. salt
1 tbs. sugar
1/2 cup pineapple juice
1/4 cup papaya juice
1/4 cup butter or margarine, melted and cooled

Beat egg white in a small bowl until stiff and set aside. Mix together dry ingredients and set aside. Combine egg yolk, juices, and butter. Add to dry ingredients, mixing until just blended. Fold in beaten egg white until just mixed. Do not overbeat batter.

CRANAPPLE WAFFLES

The small pieces of apple and cranberry lend lots of great texture and taste to this distinctive waffle. A favorite combination.

1 egg, room temperature and
  separated
1 cup all-purpose flour
1 tsp. baking powder
1/8 tsp. salt
1 tbs. sugar
1/8 tsp. cinnamon

2/3 cup cranapple, cranberry or apple
  juice
1/4 medium apple, peeled and diced
1/4 cup chopped cranberries
1/4 cup butter or margarine, melted
  and cooled
2–3 tbs. chopped nuts, optional

Beat egg white in a small bowl until stiff and set aside. Mix together dry ingredients and set aside. Combine egg yolk, juice, apple, cranberries and butter. Add to dry ingredients, mixing until just blended. Add nuts and fold in with beaten egg white until just mixed. Do not overbeat batter.

BANANA PINEAPPLE WAFFLES

These waffles have the flavor of a tropical island delight.

1 egg, room temperature and separated
1 cup all-purpose flour
1 tsp. baking powder
$1/8$ tsp. salt
1 tbs. sugar
$1/2$ cup pineapple juice
$1/4$ cup crushed pineapple, drained
$1/2$ cup mashed banana (about 1 medium banana)
$1/4$ cup butter or margarine, melted and cooled
2–3 tbs. chopped macadamias or walnuts, optional

Beat egg white in a small bowl until stiff and set aside. Mix together dry ingredients and set aside. Combine egg yolk, juice, pineapple, banana and butter. Add to dry ingredients, mixing until just blended. Add nuts, if desired, and fold in with beaten egg white until just mixed. Do not overbeat batter.

ORANGE APPLE WAFFLES

You'll love this one!

1 egg, room temperature and separated
1 cup all-purpose flour
1 tsp. baking powder
1/8 tsp. salt
1 tbs. sugar
1/4 tsp. orange peel
1/2 cup apple juice
1/2 cup Mandarin orange segments
1/4 cup butter or margarine, melted and cooled

Beat egg white in a small bowl until stiff and set aside.
Mix together dry ingredients and set aside. Combine egg yolk,
juice, orange segments and butter. Add to dry ingredients, mixing until just blended. Fold in beaten egg white until just mixed. Do not overbeat batter.

PINEAPPLE, STRAWBERRY AND BANANA WAFFLES 3 waffles

Here's another wonderful, fruity waffle that you're going to love.

1 egg, room temperature and separated
1 cup all-purpose flour
1 tsp. baking powder
1/8 tsp. salt
1 tbs. sugar
1 medium banana, mashed
1/4 cup strawberry puree
1/4 cup pineapple juice
1/4 cup butter or margarine, melted and cooled

Beat egg white in a small bowl until stiff and set aside. Mix together dry ingredients and set aside. Combine egg yolk, banana, strawberry puree, juice and butter. Add to dry ingredients, mixing until just blended. Fold in beaten egg white until just mixed. Do not over-beat batter.

PINEAPPLE ORANGE MINT WAFFLES

The aroma of mint will have people standing in line for these waffles.

1 egg, room temperature and separated
1 cup all-purpose flour
1 tsp. baking powder
$1/8$ tsp. salt
1 tbs. sugar
$1/4$ tsp. dried mint leaves or $3/4$ tsp. fresh crushed leaves
$2/3$ cup orange juice
$1/4$ cup crushed pineapple, drained
$1/2$ tsp. mint extract
$1/4$ cup butter or margarine, melted and cooled

Beat egg white in a small bowl until stiff and set aside. Mix together dry ingredients and set aside. Combine egg yolk, juice, pineapple, mint extract and butter. Add to dry ingredients, mixing until just blended. Fold in beaten egg white until just mixed. Do not overbeat batter.

WEST INDIAN BANANA WAFFLES

A truly irresistible, sweet waffle. This is one of our absolute favorites.

1 egg, room temperature and
  separated
1 cup all-purpose flour
1 tsp. baking powder
1/8 tsp. salt
1 tbs. sugar
1/4 tsp. cinnamon

1/8 tsp. nutmeg
1/2 cup canned coconut milk
1 medium banana, mashed
1 tsp. coconut extract
1/4 cup butter or margarine, melted
  and cooled
1 tbs. coconut flakes

Beat egg white in a small bowl until stiff and set aside. Mix together dry ingredients and set aside. Combine egg yolk, milk, banana, coconut extract and butter. Add to dry ingredients, mixing until just blended. Fold in coconut flakes and beaten egg white until just mixed. Do not overbeat batter.

PUMPKIN WAFFLES

This flavorful pumpkin treat is best if cooked longer so it's nice and crispy.

1 egg, room temperature and separated
1/2 cup all-purpose flour
3/4 cup oats, regular or quick cooking
1 tsp. baking powder
1/8 tsp. salt
1 tbs. brown sugar
1/4 tsp. pumpkin pie spice

1/3 cup milk
1/2 cup canned or cooked, pureed pumpkin
1/4 cup butter or margarine, melted and cooled
1/4 cup chopped walnuts or pecans, optional

Beat egg white in a small bowl until stiff and set aside. Mix together dry ingredients and set aside. Combine egg yolk, milk, pumpkin and butter. Add to dry ingredients, mixing until just blended. Add nuts and fold in with beaten egg white until just mixed. Do not overbeat batter.

CINNAMON RAISIN WAFFLES

You'll love this light, crisp waffle from the first bite.

1 egg, room temperature and separated
1 1/4 cups all-purpose flour
1 tsp. baking powder
1/8 tsp. salt
1 tbs. brown sugar
1/2 tsp. cinnamon
3/4 cup milk
1/4 cup butter or margarine, melted and cooled
1/4–1/3 cup raisins
1/4 cup chopped walnuts or pecans, optional

Beat egg white in a small bowl until stiff and set aside. Mix together dry ingredients and set aside. Combine egg yolk, milk and butter. Add to dry ingredients, mixing until just blended. Add nuts, if desired, and fold in with beaten egg white until just mixed. Do not overbeat batter.

NUT AND NUT BUTTER WAFFLES

83   Nut Waffles
84   Orange Nut Waffles
85   Honey Nut Oatmeal Waffles
86   Almond Butter Waffles
87   Peanut Butter Waffles
88   Almond Amaretto Waffles
89   Cinnamon Chocolate Nut Waffles
90   Pistachio Waffles
91   Date Nut Waffles
92   Chocolate Raisin Nut Waffles
93   Chocolate Nut Waffles
94   Brazil Nut Orange Waffles
95   Almond Apricot Waffles
96   Chocolate Almond Waffles

NUT WAFFLES

The walnut oil with walnuts is absolutely divine. Use your favorite nut — each has its own distinct taste and flavor. Suggested nuts: walnuts, almonds, pecans, brazil nuts, macadamia nuts, hazelnuts, sunflower kernels, even mixed nuts!

1 egg, room temperature and separated
1 1/4 cups all-purpose or whole wheat flour
1 tsp. baking powder
1/8 tsp. salt
1 tbs. brown sugar
3/4 cup milk
1/4 cup butter or margarine, melted, or walnut oil
1/3 cup chopped nuts

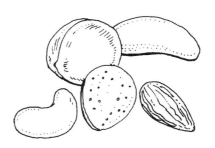

Beat egg white in a small bowl until stiff and set aside. Mix together dry ingredients and set aside. Combine egg yolk, milk and butter. Add to dry ingredients, mixing until just blended. Add nuts and fold in with beaten egg white until just mixed. Do not overbeat batter.

ORANGE NUT WAFFLES

This waffle will forever change your previous thoughts and expectations of waffles. This is a "must try."

1 egg, room temperature and separated
1 cup all-purpose flour
1 tsp. baking powder
1/8 tsp. salt
1 tbs. sugar
1/8 tsp. orange peel
3/4 cup orange juice
1/4 cup butter or margarine, melted and cooled
1/4–1/3 cup ground walnuts or pecans

Beat egg white in a small bowl until stiff and set aside. Mix together dry ingredients and set aside. Combine egg yolk, orange juice and melted butter. Add to dry ingredients, mixing until just blended. Add nuts and fold in with beaten egg white until just mixed. Do not overbeat batter.

HONEY NUT OATMEAL WAFFLES

The combination of honey, nuts and oatmeal has become a favorite in everything from cereal to bread. It shall now become a favorite of yours in waffles too! Bake longer for a crispier result.

1 egg, room temperature and separated
1/2 cup all-purpose flour
3/4 cup oats
1 tsp. baking powder
1/8 tsp. salt
3/4 cup milk
2 tbs. honey
1/4 cup butter, melted and cooled
1/4–1/3 cup chopped walnuts or pecans

Beat egg white in a small bowl until stiff and set aside. Mix together dry ingredients and set aside. Combine egg yolk, milk, honey and melted butter. Add to dry ingredients, mixing until just blended. Add nuts and fold in with beaten egg white until just mixed. Do not overbeat batter.

ALMOND BUTTER WAFFLES

This sweet, buttery waffle has lots of almond flavor.

1 egg, room temperature and separated
1 cup all-purpose flour
1 tsp. baking powder
1/8 tsp. salt
2 tbs. sugar
2/3 cup milk
2 tsp. almond extract
6 tbs. butter or margarine, melted and cooled
1/4–1/3 cup chopped almonds

Beat egg white in a small bowl until stiff and set aside. Mix together dry ingredients and set aside. Combine egg yolk, milk, almond extract and melted butter. Add to dry ingredients, mixing until just blended. Add chopped almonds and fold in with beaten egg white until just mixed. Do not overbeat batter.

PEANUT BUTTER WAFFLES

Kids of all ages flip over this. Serve with Peanut Butter and Honey Topping, *page 140, or any of the other honey spreads, pages 139 to 141.*

1 egg, room temperature and separated
1 cup all-purpose flour
1 tsp. baking powder
1/8 tsp. salt
3/4 cup milk
1/3 cup peanut butter
2 tbs. butter or margarine, melted and cooled
1 tbs. honey
1/4 cup chocolate chips, optional

Beat egg white in a small bowl until stiff and set aside. Mix together dry ingredients and set aside. Combine egg yolk, milk, peanut butter, honey and butter. Add to dry ingredients, mixing until just blended. Fold in chocolate chips, if desired, and beaten egg white until just mixed. Do not overbeat batter.

ALMOND AMARETTO WAFFLES

Here's a truly festive way to start a leisurely day.

1 egg, room temperature and separated
1 1/4 cups all-purpose flour
1 tsp. baking powder
1/8 tsp. salt
1 tbs. brown sugar
1/3 cup amaretto
1/2 cup milk
1/4 cup butter or margarine, melted and cooled
1/4 cup chopped almonds

Beat egg white in a small bowl until stiff and set aside. Mix together dry ingredients and set aside. Combine egg yolk, amaretto, milk and butter. Add to dry ingredients, mixing until just blended. Add nuts and fold in with beaten egg white until just mixed. Do not overbeat batter.

CINNAMON CHOCOLATE NUT WAFFLES

The combination of cinnamon and chocolate is often found in Mexican cooking. Ole! If desired, nuts can, of course, be omitted.

1 egg, room temperature and separated
1 1/4 cups all-purpose flour
1 tsp. baking powder
1/8 tsp. salt
3 tbs. sugar
1/4 tsp. cinnamon
2 tbs. unsweetened cocoa
3/4 cup milk
1/4 cup butter or margarine, melted and cooled
1/4 cup chopped walnuts

Beat egg white in a small bowl until stiff and set aside. Mix together dry ingredients and set aside. Combine egg yolk, milk and butter. Add to dry ingredients, mixing until just blended. Add nuts and fold in with beaten egg white until just mixed. Do not overbeat batter.

PISTACHIO WAFFLES

These light, crispy waffles have a delicate flavoring of pistachios.

1 egg, room temperature and separated
1 cup all-purpose flour
1 tsp. baking powder
1/8 tsp. salt
1 tbs. sugar
3/4 cup milk
1 tsp. almond extract
1/4 cup butter or margarine, melted and cooled
1/4–1/3 cup very finely chopped pistachios
2 tbs. raisins, optional

Beat egg white in a small bowl until stiff and set aside. Mix together dry ingredients and set aside. Combine egg yolk, milk, almond extract and butter. Add to dry ingredients, mixing until just blended. Add nuts, and raisins if desired; fold in with beaten egg white until just mixed. Do not overbeat batter.

DATE NUT WAFFLES

Some testers preferred this sweet, cake-like waffle without any syrup.

1 egg, room temperature and separated
1 1/4 cups all-purpose flour
1 tsp. baking powder
1/8 tsp. salt
1 1/2 tsp. unsweetened cocoa
3/4 cup milk
1 tbs. molasses
1/4 cup butter or margarine, melted and cooled
1/4 cup chopped dates
1/4 cup chopped walnuts

Beat egg white in a small bowl until stiff and set aside. Mix together dry ingredients and set aside. Combine egg yolk, milk, molasses and melted butter. Add to dry ingredients, mixing until just blended. Add dates and nuts; fold in with beaten egg white until just mixed. Do not overbeat batter.

NUT AND NUT BUTTER WAFFLES   91

CHOCOLATE RAISIN NUT WAFFLES

3 waffles

What a great combination. You may never return to plain waffles again!

1 egg, room temperature and separated
1 cup all-purpose flour
1 tsp. baking powder
1/8 tsp. salt
1 tbs. brown sugar
1 1/2 tsp. unsweetened cocoa
3/4 cup milk
1/4 cup butter or margarine, melted and cooled
1/4–1/3 cup raisins
1/4 cup chopped walnuts or pecans

Beat egg white in a small bowl until stiff and set aside. Mix together dry ingredients and set aside. Combine egg yolk, milk and melted butter. Add to dry ingredients, mixing until just blended. Add raisins and nuts; fold in with beaten egg white until just mixed. Do not overbeat batter.

CHOCOLATE NUT WAFFLES

This is an outrageously decadent chocolate waffle. Serve it with chocolate or maple syrup or as a dessert with ice cream.

1 egg, room temperature and separated
1 1/4 cups all-purpose flour
1 tsp. baking powder
1/8 tsp. salt
1/4 cup sweetened chocolate powder
3/4 cup milk
1/4 cup butter or margarine, melted and cooled
1/4–1/3 cup chopped nuts
1/4–1/3 cup chocolate chips, optional

Beat egg white in a small bowl until stiff and set aside. Mix together dry ingredients and set aside. Combine egg yolk, milk and butter. Add to dry ingredients, mixing until just blended. Add nuts and chocolate chips, if desired, and fold in with beaten egg white until just mixed. Do not overbeat batter.

Note: Sweetened chocolate powder is often sold as a hot chocolate powder mix.

BRAZIL NUT ORANGE WAFFLES

The combination of milk and orange juice is superb. Brazil nuts give these waffles pizzazz.

1 egg, room temperature and separated
1 cup all-purpose flour
1 tsp. baking powder
$1/8$ tsp. salt
1 tbs. brown sugar
$1/2$ cup orange juice
$1/4$ cup milk
$1/4$ cup butter or margarine, melted and cooled
$1/4$–$1/3$ cup chopped brazil nuts

Beat egg white in a small bowl until stiff and set aside. Mix together dry ingredients and set aside. Combine egg yolk, juice, milk and butter. Add to dry ingredients, mixing until just blended. Add nuts and fold in with beaten egg white until just mixed. Do not overbeat batter.

ALMOND APRICOT WAFFLES

A must for apricot lovers, this is a unique, flavorful waffle.

1 egg, room temperature and
   separated
1 cup all-purpose flour
1/3 cup oats
1 tsp. baking powder
1/8 tsp. salt
1/16 tsp. grated lemon peel
3/4 cup milk

1/2 tsp. almond extract
1 tbs. honey
1/4 cup butter or margarine, melted
   and cooled
2–3 tbs. diced dried apricots
2–3 tbs. chopped almonds
1–2 tbs. raisins, optional

Beat egg white in a small bowl until stiff and set aside. Mix together dry ingredients and set aside. Combine egg yolk, milk, almond extract, honey and butter. Add to dry ingredients, mixing until just blended. Add apricots, nuts, and raisins if desired; fold in with beaten egg white until just mixed. Do not overbeat batter.

CHOCOLATE ALMOND WAFFLES

Wow — this is out of this world. Not for a day you are trying to diet!

1 egg, room temperature and
   separated
1 cup all-purpose flour
1 tsp. baking powder
1/8 tsp. salt
1/8 tsp. cinnamon
1/16 tsp. allspice

1/4 cup sweetened chocolate powder
2/3 cup milk
1 tbs. almond extract
1/4 cup butter or margarine melted and
   cooled
1/4–1/3 cup chopped almonds
1/4–1/3 cup chocolate chips, optional

Beat egg white in a small bowl until stiff and set aside. Mix together dry ingredients and set aside. Combine egg yolk, milk, almond extract and butter. Add to dry ingredients, mixing until just blended. Add nuts and chocolate chips; fold in with beaten egg white until just mixed. Do not overbeat batter.

Note: Sweetened chocolate powder is often sold as a hot chocolate powder mix.

YEAST WAFFLES

ABOUT YEAST WAFFLES

Waffles, just as many other baked foods, require a leavening agent. Most people assume that such an agent in waffle making must be the baking powder. Yeast has also been used, on occasion, in waffle making. You may be asking yourself why yeast should be used when it may seem like a lot of bother to proof it, etc. I found, during the testing for this book, that I actually preferred the yeast waffles and that they were easier to make on rushed mornings! The majority of the batter is made the evening before and all that needs to be done in the morning is to add the egg and in some cases, baking soda.

Please try at least one yeast waffle — don't let it scare you. Proofing the yeast sounds intimidating, but it really is as easy as sprinkling the yeast granules over lukewarm water (105° to 110°). You need not actually use a thermometer to determine if the water is the right temperature — just put a few drops on the inside of your wrist and see if it is comfortably warm. Then sprinkle the yeast granules on top of the measured water (I do this in the bowl in which I will make the batter), cover it with a kitchen towel and set it aside for about 5 minutes while preparing the other ingredients.

BASIC YEAST WAFFLES

This is a wonderful variation on a basic waffle. Just a small amount of yeast makes these waffles rise nicely.

1/4 cup lukewarm water (105°–110°)
1/2 tsp. yeast
1 cup all-purpose flour
1/8 tsp. salt

1 tsp. sugar
1/2 cup milk, lukewarm
1/4 cup butter, melted and cooled to
   room temperature

——

1 egg, room temperature and separated   1/8 tsp. baking soda

Proof yeast in warm water for about 5 minutes. At the same time, mix together dry ingredients and set aside. Add milk and butter to yeast mixture. Add dry ingredients, mixing until just blended. Cover bowl with kitchen towel or plastic wrap and set in your cool oven or other draft-free location overnight.

In the morning, beat egg white in a small bowl until stiff and set aside. Mix egg yolk and baking soda into batter and stir in egg white until just blended. Cook as usual.

YEASTED ORANGE NUT WAFFLES

Yeast provides a delightful twist to an old favorite.

¹/₄ cup lukewarm water (105°–110°)
¹/₂ tsp. yeast
1 cup all-purpose flour
¹/₈ tsp. salt
1 tsp. sugar

¹/₈ tsp. orange peel
¹/₂ cup orange juice, lukewarm
 (105°–110°)
¹/₄ cup butter, melted and cooled to
 room temperature

——

1 egg, room temperature and
 separated

¹/₄ cup chopped nuts (walnuts, pecans,
 or almonds)

Proof yeast in warm water for about 5 minutes. At the same time, mix together dry ingredients and set aside. Add orange juice and butter to yeast mixture. Add dry ingredients, mixing until just blended. Cover bowl with kitchen towel or plastic wrap and set in your cool oven or other draft-free location overnight.

In the morning, beat egg white in a small bowl until stiff and set aside. Mix egg yolk and nuts into batter and stir in egg white until just blended. Cook as usual.

YEASTED HONEY NUT OATMEAL WAFFLES

This is a delightful, sweet and nutty waffle.

3/4 cup lukewarm water (105°–110°)
1/2 tsp. yeast
3/4 cup all-purpose flour
3/4 cup oats, regular or quick cooking

1/4–1/2 tsp. salt
2 tbs. honey
1/4 cup butter, melted and cooled to
   room temperature

— —

1 egg, room temperature and
   separated

1/4 cup chopped nuts (walnuts, pecans,
   or almonds)

Proof yeast in warm water for about 5 minutes. At the same time, mix together dry ingredients and set aside. Add honey and butter to yeast mixture. Add dry ingredients, mixing until just blended. Cover bowl with kitchen towel or plastic wrap and set in your cool oven or other draft-free location overnight.

In the morning, beat egg white in a small bowl until stiff and set aside. Mix egg yolk and nuts into batter and stir in egg white until just blended. Cook as usual.

YEASTED LEMON WAFFLES

This recipe makes a very light, crispy and terrific waffle. Serve with lemon curd (may be warmed in the microwave) or Lemon Cream, page 142. This is sure to become a favorite. Do not cook too long.

⅔ cup lukewarm water (105°–110°)	1 tsp. grated lemon peel
½ tsp. yeast	2 tbs. lemon juice
1 cup all-purpose flour	¼ cup butter, melted and cooled to
¼ tsp. salt	room temperature
1 tbs. sugar	

— —

1 egg, room temperature and separated

Proof yeast in warm water for about 5 minutes. At the same time, mix together dry ingredients and set aside. Add juice and butter to yeast mixture. Add dry ingredients, mixing until just blended. Cover bowl with kitchen towel or plastic wrap and set in your cool oven or other draft-free location overnight.

In the morning, beat egg white in a small bowl until stiff and set aside. Mix egg yolk into batter and stir in egg white until just blended. Cook as usual.

YEASTED WHIPPED CREAM WAFFLES

This light, fluffy and truly rich waffle is not meant for calorie counting. Do not overcook.

1/4 cup lukewarm water (105°–110°)
1/2 tsp. yeast
1 cup all-purpose flour
1/4 tsp. salt
1/4 tsp. grated orange or lemon peel

1/2 cup whipping cream or heavy cream
2 tbs. confectioners' sugar
1/4 cup butter, melted and cooled to
    room temperature

— —

1 egg, room temperature and separated   1/8 tsp. baking soda

Proof yeast in warm water for about 5 minutes. At the same time, whip cream and confectioners' sugar until thick. Mix together dry ingredients and set aside. Add whipped cream and butter to yeast mixture. Add dry ingredients, mixing until just blended. Cover bowl with kitchen towel or plastic wrap and set in your cool oven or other draft-free location overnight.

In the morning, beat egg white in a small bowl until stiff and set aside. Mix egg yolk and baking soda into batter and stir in egg white until just blended. Cook as usual.

CHRISTMAS MORNING WAFFLES

As the batter is made the evening before, this makes THE PERFECT breakfast for Christmas morning — a wonderful, festive waffle with minimal morning preparation. For real "eye appeal" use both red and green cherries which are available during the holiday season.

1/4 cup lukewarm water (105°–110°)
1/2 tsp. yeast
1 cup all-purpose flour
1/8 tsp. salt
1/5 tsp. nutmeg
1 tbs. confectioners' sugar
2/3 cup eggnog
2 tbs. butter, melted and cooled to room temperature
— —
1 egg, room temperature and separated
1/8 tsp. baking soda
1/4 cup maraschino cherries (about 10)
2 tbs. chopped nuts (any kind)

Proof yeast in warm water for about 5 minutes. At the same time, mix together dry ingredients and set aside. Add eggnog and butter to yeast mixture. Add dry ingredients, mixing until just blended. Cover bowl with kitchen towel or plastic wrap and set in your cool oven or other draft-free location overnight.

In the morning, beat egg white in a small bowl until stiff and set aside. Mix egg yolk, baking soda, cherries and nuts into batter and stir in egg white until just blended. Cook as usual.

YEASTED HOMESTYLE WAFFLES

You'll enjoy this light and airy buttermilk waffle.

¹/₄ cup lukewarm water (105°–110°)
¹/₂ tsp. yeast
1 cup all-purpose flour
¹/₈ tsp. salt
2 tsp. sugar

¹/₄ tsp. grated orange or lemon peel
²/₃ cup buttermilk
2 tbs. butter, melted and cooled to
   room temperature

——

1 egg, room temperature and separated   ¹/₈ tsp. baking soda

Proof yeast in warm water for about 5 minutes. At the same time, mix together dry ingredients and set aside. Add buttermilk and butter to yeast mixture. Add dry ingredients, mixing until just blended. Cover bowl with kitchen towel or plastic wrap and set in your cool oven or other draft-free location overnight.

In the morning, beat egg white in a small bowl until stiff and set aside. Mix egg yolk and baking soda into batter and stir in egg white until just blended. Cook as usual.

YEASTED WHOLE WHEAT AND BRAN WAFFLES

Use this nutritious waffle for sandwiches or as a base for creamed chicken for a supper.

3/4 cup lukewarm water (105°–110°)
1/2 tsp. yeast
1 cup whole wheat flour
1/4 cup bran (oat, wheat or rice)

1/8 tsp. salt
1/4 cup butter, melted and cooled to
   room temperature
1 tbs. honey

— —

1 egg, room temperature and separated

Proof yeast in warm water for about 5 minutes. At the same time, mix together dry ingredients and set aside. Add honey and butter to yeast mixture. Add dry ingredients, mixing until just blended. Cover bowl with kitchen towel or plastic wrap and set in your cool oven or other draft-free location overnight.

In the morning, beat egg white in a small bowl until stiff and set aside. Mix egg yolk into batter and stir in egg white until just blended. Cook as usual.

YEASTED BUCKWHEAT OATMEAL WAFFLES

3 waffles

Here's a must for buckwheat lovers. The combination of buckwheat and oatmeal is an old favorite of many.

1/4 cup lukewarm water (105°–110°)
1/2 tsp. yeast
1/2 cup buckwheat flour
1 cup oats, regular or quick cooking
1/8 tsp. salt

1/2 cup milk, lukewarm (105°–110°)
1/4 cup butter, melted and cooled to
    room temperature
2 tbs. honey

— —

1 egg, room temperature and separated   1/8 tsp. baking soda

Proof yeast in water for about 5 minutes. At the same time, mix together dry ingredients and set aside. Add milk, honey and butter to yeast mixture. Add dry ingredients, mixing until just blended. Cover bowl with kitchen towel or plastic wrap and set in your cool oven or other draft-free location overnight.

In the morning, beat egg white in a small bowl until stiff and set aside. Mix egg yolk and baking soda into batter and stir in egg white until just blended. Cook as usual.

PIZZELLES

DIRECTIONS FOR MAKING PIZZELLES

Pizzelles can be served or eaten fresh off the heat, cooled and enjoyed plain (as "cookies"), or shaped into cannolis, bowls or waffle cones.

Each pizzelle recipe in this chapter makes about two dozen 4-inch cookies. All recipes can be easily doubled or tripled. A waffle cone maker can be used to make any of these recipes, but will make larger cookies, hence a smaller number.

When making the dough, add flour or water a tablespoon at a time to adjust the consistency, if required. The dough should fall off a spoon onto the baking surface.

Heat the pizzelle maker properly and use a teflon-coated spatula to lift the cookies off. If shaping the cookies, remove one cookie at a time and shape immediately. Do not overcook cookies that will be shaped. Allow cookies to cool on a rack or paper towels. Store in plastic containers.

Do not wash pizzelle maker; simply brush off with a paper towel when cool.

SHAPING PIZZELLES

Cannolis (cylinders): Remove the hot pizzelle from the cooker and wrap immediately around a wooden dowel or spoon handle. For best results, remove one cookie at a time. It will take a little practice at first, but any failed attempts still make great eating. Place the overlapped area flat on the counter and press down to seal while pizzelle cools, about 5 to 10 seconds. The size of the dowel will determine the size of the cylinder. I recommend using a dowel between $1/2$ inch and 1 inch in diameter. Your decision, however, will depend on the size of the cookies you are wrapping, and whether you will be stuffing or dipping the cylinders.

To stuff cylinders, load filling into a pastry bag or locking plastic bag. Cut off one corner of bag and fill cylinders completely by squeezing filling into the shell. Refrigerate filled cookies for a few minutes to set filling.

Bowls: Place warm cookie over an upside-down bowl or glass or into muffin tins. Push down to shape. Cool at room temperature for a few minutes. Bowls can be used to serve anything from ice cream or pudding to fresh fruit and whipped cream. Savory bowls can be used to serve small salads.

Waffle Cones: Wrap warm pizzelles around a wooden or plastic cone (available in some kitchen shops or craft stores). Press the overlapping section onto the counter by holding down with the cone shape with one hand. Seal the bottom of the cone by pressing down with fingers at the same time. Cool at room temperature for a minute or two.

Swirled Pizzelles: Make two different pizzelle doughs, usually one a chocolate dough because of the visual difference. Take half your spoonful from each batter and drop onto the pizzelle maker. Cook according to manufacturer's directions. Suggested combinations include orange and chocolate, mint and chocolate, or just about anything and chocolate!

BASIC SWEET PIZZELLES

Makes 18

This basic recipe may be used as a base for any topping or filling. Or, simply dust with confectioners' sugar and enjoy. This is a basic waffle cone recipe too.

3 eggs
1/2 cup butter, softened
1 tbs. vanilla extract
3/4 cup granulated sugar
1 1/2 tsp. baking powder
1 1/2 cups all-purpose flour

Beat eggs and add softened butter, vanilla and sugar, beating until creamy. Add baking powder to flour and beat flour mixture into egg mixture. Bake according to manufacturer's instructions.

VARIATIONS

Vanilla Pizzelles: Slice vanilla bean in half and scrape inside into batter. Increase vanilla extract to 2 tbs. and scrape inside of about 2 inches vanilla bean. Beat in with egg mixture. The extra vanilla gives a flavorful boost to accompany flavored coffees. These make perfect bowls with fresh strawberries and/or blueberries and whipped cream.

Mint Pizzelles: Replace vanilla with 2 tbs. mint or peppermint extract. Add ¼ cup mini-chocolate chips if desired. What a wonderful bowl or waffle cone with mint chocolate chip ice cream! Or, make a cylinder, dip into melted chocolate and serve with ice cream or after-dinner coffee. Fill cylinders with *Chocolate Fruit Nut Filling*, page 147, using orange marmalade.

Coffee Pizzelles: Substitute coffee liqueur for vanilla extract. Add 2 tbs. instant coffee grounds. Delicious served as is, or as a cylinder dipped in chocolate with a cup of coffee.

Spiced Pizzelles: Add one of the following: 1 tbs. pumpkin pie spice, apple pie spice, cinnamon, nutmeg or allspice, to the flour mixture. Depending on how or with what they are served, pick your flavoring. Serve cinnamon pizzelles dusted with cinnamon sugar (a kids' favorite), or the apple or pumpkin pie spice in the fall with hot cider. Or, make *Flavored Cream Filling*, page 148, using the same seasoning as the pizzelle.

EASY CHOCOLATE PIZZELLES

This quick and easy chocolate pizzelle goes well with any type of ice cream or pudding. Try swirling it with any plain, vanilla or nut pizzelles for a festive presentation.

3 eggs
$1/2$ cup butter, softened
1 tbs. vanilla extract
1 cup granulated sugar

$1 1/2$ tsp. baking powder
$1/4$ cup cocoa
$1 1/2$ cups all-purpose flour
$1/4$ cup mini-chocolate chips, optional

Beat eggs and add softened butter, vanilla and sugar, beating until creamy. Add cocoa and baking powder to flour and beat flour mixture into egg mixture. Stir in mini-chocolate chips, if using. Bake according to manufacturer's instructions.

Variation: CHOCOLATE COCONUT PIZZELLES

Roll pizzelles into cylinders. Dip one end into melted chocolate and sprinkle with coconut flakes. Serve with ice cream, sherbet or coconut custard.

Or, substitute coconut extract for the vanilla and add $1/4$ cup shredded, sweetened coconut.

DECADENT CHOCOLATE PIZZELLES

Makes 18

This requires a little extra work but is well worth it. Serve with orange sherbet (use orange extract), coconut custard (use coconut extract) or fresh strawberries.

$1/2$ cup butter
$1/2$ cup chocolate chips
3 eggs
1 tbs. vanilla, orange or coconut extract
$3/4$ cup granulated sugar
2 tsp. baking powder
$1\frac{1}{2}$ cups all-purpose flour

In a small pan, melt butter and chocolate chips, stirring constantly. Remove from heat and let cool. Beat eggs and add cooled butter-chocolate mixture, vanilla extract and sugar, beating until creamy. Add baking powder to flour and beat flour mixture into egg mixture. Bake according to manufacturer's instructions.

Variation: WHITE CHOCOLATE MACADAMIA NUT PIZZELLES
Use white chocolate chips and vanilla extract and add $1/4$ cup chopped macadamia nuts to flour.

ORANGE PIZZELLES

Makes 18

These are wonderful as waffle cones or "ice cream bowls" with orange sherbet. Or, use the cannoli filling with 1 tbs. orange peel. This is fun swirled with Easy Chocolate Pizzelles, *page 115, or* Decadent Chocolate Pizzelles, *page 116. If using fresh peel, use the peel of a full orange.*

3 eggs	¾ cup granulated sugar
½ cup butter, softened	1½ tsp. baking powder
1 tbs. orange extract	1½ cups all-purpose flour
1 tbs. orange peel	

Beat eggs and add softened butter, orange extract, peel and sugar, beating until creamy. Add baking powder to flour and beat flour mixture into egg mixture. Bake according to manufacturer's instructions.

Variation: ORANGE CHOCOLATE PIZZELLES

Dip cylinders into melted chocolate for an extra chocolate fix. Or, shape into cylinders and fill with *Chocolate-Fruit Nut Filling,* page 147, using orange marmalade. Or, add ¼ cup mini-chocolate chips to flour mixture.

LEMON PIZZELLES

Makes 18

Either of these cookies is superb with lemon sherbet or lemon curd. If making cannoli, add 1 tbs. lemon peel to the cannoli filing. If using fresh peel, use the peel from 2 lemons.

3 eggs
½ cup butter, softened
1 tbs. lemon extract
1 tbs. lemon zest
¾ cup granulated sugar
1½ tsp. baking powder
1½ cups all-purpose flour

Beat eggs and add softened butter, lemon extract, zest and sugar, beating until creamy. Add baking powder to flour and beat flour mixture into egg mixture. Bake according to manufacturer's instructions.

Variation: LEMON POPPY SEED PIZZELLES
Add 2 tbs. poppy seeds to flour mixture.

ORANGE CRANBERRY PIZZELLES

Makes 18

Make into bowls for orange sherbet or yogurt, or enjoy as is or as cylinders with coffee.

3 eggs
$1/2$ cup butter, softened
1 tbs. orange extract
1 tbs. orange peel
$3/4$ cup granulated sugar
$11/4$ cups all-purpose flour
$1/4$ cup dried cranberries
$1/4$ cup walnuts
$11/2$ tsp. baking powder

Beat eggs and add softened butter, orange extract, peel and sugar, beating until creamy. Put $1/4$ cup of the flour, cranberries and nuts into a food processor workbowl and chop. The flour helps to keep cranberries from sticking together. Add baking powder to remaining flour and cranberry-nut mixture. Beat flour mixture into egg mixture. Bake according to manufacturer's instructions.

PIZZELLES   119

CINNAMON RAISIN PIZZELLES

If using as cannoli, add 1 tbs. cinnamon to the Cannoli Filling, *page 149.*

3 eggs
1/2 cup butter, softened
1 tbs. vanilla extract
1 tbs. cinnamon
3/4 cup granulated sugar
1 1/4 cups all-purpose flour
1/4 cup raisins
1/4 cup walnuts
1 1/2 tsp. baking powder

Beat eggs and add softened butter, vanilla extract, cinnamon and sugar, beating until creamy. Put 1/4 cup of the flour, raisins and nuts into a food processor work-bowl and chop. The flour helps to keep raisins from sticking together. Add baking powder to remaining flour and raisin-nut mixture. Beat flour mixture into egg mixture. Bake according to manufacturer's instructions.

CHOCOLATE CHERRY PIZZELLES

This is wonderful with cherry vanilla yogurt or ice cream. If dried cherries are difficult to find, try using cherry-flavored dried cranberries.

3 eggs
$1/2$ cup butter, softened
1 tbs. cherry extract
1 cup granulated sugar
$1 1/4$ cups all-purpose flour
$1/4$ cup dried cherries
$1 1/2$ tsp. baking powder
$1/4$ cup cocoa

Beat eggs and add softened butter, cherry extract and sugar, beating until creamy. Put $1/4$ cup of the flour and cherries into a food processor workbowl and chop. The flour helps to keep cherries from sticking together. Add baking powder and cocoa to remaining flour and cherry mixture. Beat flour mixture into egg mixture. Bake according to manufacturer's instructions.

BANANA NUT PIZZELLES

This very flavorful cookie is good as is or shaped as a bowl and filled with banana pudding. If making pudding, add 1 tsp. banana extract to a vanilla pudding mix. Make pudding, cool and fill bowls after pudding has set. Top with sliced bananas and whipped cream.

3 eggs
1 medium-sized ripe banana
$1/2$ cup butter, softened
1 tbs. banana extract
$3/4$ cup granulated sugar
$1 1/2$ tsp. baking powder
$1 3/4$ cups all-purpose flour
$1/4$ cup finely ground walnuts or macadamia nuts

Beat eggs and add banana, softened butter, banana extract and sugar, beating until creamy. Add baking powder to flour and nuts and beat flour mixture into egg mixture. Add flour or water if necessary until batter is soft enough to be dropped by spoon. Bake according to manufacturer's instructions.

PINEAPPLE PIZZELLES

Makes 18

Either of these is wonderful served with coconut custard, fresh tropical fruit or fruit sherbet.

2 eggs
½ cup butter, softened
1 can (8¼ oz.) crushed pineapple, drained
1 tbs. vanilla or pineapple extract
½ cup granulated sugar
1½ tsp. baking powder
¼ cup ground macadamia nuts
1¼ cups all-purpose flour

Beat eggs and add softened butter, pineapple, extract and sugar, beating until creamy. Add baking powder and nuts to flour. Beat flour mixture into egg mixture. Bake according to manufacturer's instructions.

Variation: PINEAPPLE COCONUT PIZZELLES
Add ¼ cup sweetened shredded coconut.

ANISE PIZZELLES

This is a very traditional Italian pizzelle. Serve as is or dusted with confectioners' sugar with coffee or cappuccino.

3 eggs
1/2 cup butter, softened
2 tbs. anise extract
1 tbs. anise seed
3/4 cup granulated sugar
1 1/2 tsp. baking powder
1 1/2 cups all-purpose flour

Beat eggs and add softened butter, extract, anise seeds and sugar, beating until creamy. Add baking powder to flour and beat flour mixture into egg mixture. Bake according to manufacturer's instructions.

ALMOND POPPY SEED PIZZELLES

Serve with lemon sherbet for a real treat! Or, make into cylinders and fill with Creamy Preserve Filling, page 146, with apricot preserves. Omit poppy seeds for a plain almond pizzelle.

3 eggs
$1/2$ cup butter, softened
2 tbs. almond extract
$3/4$ cup granulated sugar
$1 1/2$ tsp. baking powder
2 tbs. poppy seeds
$1/4$ cup finely chopped almonds
$1 1/2$ cups all-purpose flour

Beat eggs and add softened butter, almond extract and sugar, beating until creamy. Add baking powder, poppy seeds and nuts to flour. Beat flour mixture into egg mixture. Bake according to manufacturer's instructions.

FAVORITE LIQUEUR PIZZELLES

Makes 18

Use your favorite liqueur or cordial in this recipe. Serve with after-dinner drinks or flavored coffee to top off a great meal. Suggestions include amaretto, Grand Marnier, anisette, or framboise. Flavored rum goes well too. The stronger the flavor of liqueur, the stronger flavor of the pizzelle.

2 eggs	$3/4$ cup granulated sugar
$1/2$ cup butter, softened	$1 1/2$ tsp. baking powder
$1/4$ cup liqueur, cordial or rum	$1 1/2$ cups all-purpose flour

Beat eggs and add softened butter, liqueur, and sugar, beating until creamy. Add baking powder to flour and beat flour mixture into egg mixture. Add flour if necessary until batter is stiff enough to be dropped by spoon. Bake according to manufacturer's instructions.

Variation: AMARETTO ALMOND PIZZELLES

Use amaretto and add $1/4$ cup finely ground almonds. Serve with amaretto coffee for dessert or eat as is, at any time of day.

CHERRY COCONUT PIZZELLES

This recipe makes a fabulous bowl for serving cherry vanilla ice cream or yogurt or coconut custard. If using an electric mixer, the cherries will become chopped in the mixing. If mixing by hand, chop the cherries first.

3 eggs
$1/2$ cup butter, softened
4–5 maraschino cherries
1 tbs. cherry extract
1 tbs. coconut extract
$3/4$ cup granulated sugar
$1 1/2$ tsp. baking powder
$1/2$ cup shredded, sweetened coconut
$1/4$ cup finely chopped walnuts or macadamia nuts
$1 1/2$ cups all-purpose flour

Beat eggs and add softened butter, cherries, extracts and sugar, beating until creamy. Add baking powder, coconut and nuts to flour. Beat flour mixture into egg mixture. Bake according to manufacturer's instructions.

PEANUT BUTTER PIZZELLES

Kids of all ages love these, just as they are or with a simple dusting of confectioners' sugar.

2 eggs
1/4 cup peanut butter
1/2 cup butter, softened
1 tbs. vanilla extract
3/4 cup granulated sugar
1 1/2 tsp. baking powder
1 1/2 cups all-purpose flour

Beat eggs and add peanut butter, softened butter, vanilla and sugar, beating until creamy. Add baking powder to flour and beat flour mixture into egg mixture. Bake according to manufacturer's instructions.

Variation: PEANUT BUTTER CHOCOLATE CHIP PIZZELLES
Add 1/4 cup mini-chocolate chips to flour mixture.

HONEY NUT OATMEAL PIZZELLES

Makes 18–24

This very flavorful pizzelle stands alone or is great with Creamy Preserve Filling, *page 146, or* Chocolate-Fruit-Nut Filling, *page 147, using any flavor of preserve.*

2 eggs
$1/4$ cup honey
$1/2$ cup butter, softened
1 tbs. vanilla extract
1 tbs. cinnamon, optional
$1/2$ cup light brown sugar, packed
2 tsp. baking powder
1 cup all-purpose flour
1 cup quick cooking oats
$1/4$ cup finely chopped walnuts

Beat eggs and add honey, softened butter, vanilla, cinnamon and sugar, beating until creamy. Add baking powder to flour, oats and nuts. Beat flour mixture into egg mixture. Bake according to manufacturer's instructions.

KRÜM KAKKE

These Norwegian cookies are made on presses similar to pizzelle irons. They are served rolled into cylinder shapes and are often found at church potlucks and special occasions.

3 eggs
1 cup sugar
1 cup whipping cream

$1/2$ cup butter, softened
1 tsp. vanilla extract
$1 1/2$ cups all-purpose flour

Beat eggs, add sugar and beat together. Add whipping cream, butter and vanilla and beat until creamy. Add flour, mixing well. Drop by spoonfuls onto pizzelle maker; batter will be softer than a pizzelle. Roll into cylinder shapes immediately upon removing from the heat.

VARIATIONS

Cardamom Krüm Kakke: Add 1 tsp. ground cardamom to the batter.

Lemon Krüm Kakke: Add 1 tbs. lemon peel to the batter and substitute lemon extract for vanilla.

Almond Krüm Kakke: Substitute almond extract for vanilla.

HERBED PARMESAN CHEESE PIZZELLES

Makes 18

Make a savory cracker to serve with soup and salad. Spread cracker or fill cylinders with crab dip, spinach dip or lox and cream cheese. I use shredded Parmesan cheese from the deli section, not the "green can" Parmesan.

3 eggs
$1/2$ cup butter, softened
$1/2$ cup shredded fresh Parmesan cheese
$1/2$ cup granulated sugar
$1 1/2$ tsp. baking powder
2 tbs. chopped fresh parsley or chopped chives
$1 1/2$ cups all-purpose flour

Beat eggs and add softened butter, Parmesan cheese and sugar, beating until creamy. Add baking powder and herbs to flour and beat flour mixture into egg mixture. Bake according to manufacturer's instructions.

CINNAMON PECAN PIZZELLES

A great cookie alone or with pudding or ice cream. If serving as cannoli, add cinnamon to the filling.

3 eggs
$1/2$ cup butter, softened
1 tbs. vanilla extract
$1/2$ cup light brown sugar, packed
$1/4$ cup granulated sugar
$1 1/2$ tsp. baking powder
$1/2$ cup finely chopped pecans
$1 1/2$ cups all-purpose flour

Beat eggs and add softened butter, vanilla extract and sugars, beating until creamy. Add baking powder and nuts to flour. Beat flour mixture into egg mixture. Bake according to manufacturer's instructions.

TOPPINGS

TOPPING IDEAS

A walk down the grocery aisle today will provide you with a wealth of ideas for waffle and pizzelle toppings. These are some of the things you will find:

- an abundance of various fruit syrups
- applesauce
- apple butter
- confectioners' sugar — powder top
- fresh fruit — add confectioners' sugar, yogurt, or sauté in butter
- lemon curd
- creme fraiche with fresh fruit
- pourable fruit (an unsweetened fruit conserve found in health food stores or some larger grocery stores)
- sauces — chocolate, butterscotch, etc.
- ice cream
- whipped cream and fruit

In addition to sweets, try using whole grain waffles in place of rice or noodles with your favorite dinner. Some lunch or dinner suggestions to serve over waffles include:

- Welsh rarebit
- pizza (pizza sauce, mozzarella, meats and/or vegetables)
- creamed chicken or meats
- chipped beef
- Stroganoff or stews
- chili on a corn waffle
- creamed vegetables

CRANBERRY BUTTER

Prepare this butter for a festive fall treat. It can also be served with bread during your Thanksgiving meal. Shape it with a related cookie cutter by filling the cookie cutter and chilling until firm. Carefully push the butter out onto a plate or butter dish.

½ cup unsalted butter, softened
2 tbs. confectioners' sugar
⅛ tsp. orange peel
3 tbs. chopped fresh cranberries

Mix butter and confectioners' sugar in a food processor or blender until well blended. Add orange peel and cranberries and process or blend until just mixed. Shape with individual butter molds or cookie cutters, or shape into a ball. Serve chilled or at room temperature. Butter can be refrigerated for several days.

SPICY BUTTER

½ cup

This is wonderful served with any apple waffle.

½ cup butter, softened
1 tsp. honey
½ tsp. pumpkin pie spice

Combine ingredients until well blended. Serve at room temperature.

STRAWBERRY TOPPING

½ cup

This is absolutely delicious. One of the best.

4 oz. cream cheese, softened
½ cup confectioners' sugar
1 tbs. pureed strawberries

Cream softened cream cheese. Add sugar and blend well; fold in strawberries. Serve chilled or warmed in the microwave.

ORANGE TOPPING

½ cup

Serve with any basic or orange waffle. Delicious.

4 oz. cream cheese, softened
½ cup confectioners' sugar

4–5 Mandarin orange segments
⅛ tsp. orange peel

Cream softened cream cheese and blend in remaining ingredients. Serve chilled or warmed from the microwave.

SAUTÉED APPLES

Servings: 2–4

Serve with Spice Waffles, page 44, or with any apple or basic waffle. Serve with or without maple syrup.

1 medium apple, peeled and thinly
   sliced or diced

¼ tsp. cinnamon
1 tbs. butter or margarine

Melt butter or margarine in a small skillet over low heat. Add apple and cinnamon; sauté until crisp-tender.

Variation: MAPLE APPLES
Omit cinnamon and use 2 tbs. maple syrup.

BUTTERED PRESERVES

Serve this easy topping softened, at room temperature.

¼ cup unsalted butter, softened
¼ cup favorite fruit preserves (strawberry, apricot, peach, etc.)

Cream butter and add preserves until well blended. Use a food processor, a mixer or a blender.

ORANGE SYRUP

This can be made in advance and kept in the refrigerator. Warm in a microwave or in a double boiler. Or, simmer over very low heat while you prepare your waffles.

½ cup orange juice   1½ tsp. cornstarch
1 tsp. honey   ¼ cup Mandarin orange segments

Heat orange juice, honey and cornstarch over medium heat. Stir constantly until thickened. Add oranges and simmer for a few minutes or until ready to serve.

Variation: PINEAPPLE SYRUP

Substitute pineapple juice for the orange juice and drained crushed pineapple for the orange segments.

SPICED HONEY TOPPING

Add spices to honey to create a delectable syrup.

¹/₄ cup honey
¹/₂ tsp. cinnamon

¹/₈ tsp. nutmeg
¹/₈ tsp. ground cloves

Mix ingredients together and serve at room temperature. Keep refrigerated.

PAPAYA COCONUT TOPPING

Here's another tropical delight.

¹/₄ cup papaya juice
¹/₄ cup canned coconut milk
2 tbs. water

1¹/₂ tsp. cornstarch
1 tbs. coconut flakes

Heat papaya juice, coconut milk, water and cornstarch over low heat, stirring occasionally, until mixture thickens. Stir in coconut flakes until just mixed in and remove from heat. Serve warm. Can be rewarmed in the microwave.

FRUITED HONEY SYRUPS

¼ cup

Make creamy honey syrups using your favorite fruits. Use frozen fruit concentrates which have been thawed, or look for endless varieties of fruit concentrates at well-stocked health food stores.

¼ cup honey
1 tbs. fruit concentrate (orange, apple, grape, strawberry, blueberry, blackberry, raspberry)

Mix honey and fruit concentrate together and serve at room temperature. Keep refrigerated.

PEANUT BUTTER AND HONEY TOPPING

⅓ cup

Children will ask for waffles just to eat this topping! Try it with jelly in a sandwich.

¼ cup honey   2 tbs. peanut butter

Mix ingredients together and serve at room temperature. Keep refrigerated.

BANANA, PEANUT BUTTER AND HONEY TOPPING ¼ cup

This is really a variation of the peanut butter and honey. But it will not keep, so smaller proportions are provided.

2 tbs. honey   1½–2 tsp. mashed banana
1 tbs. peanut butter

Mix ingredients together and serve immediately.

PEACH AND ORANGE SYRUP 1 cup

This astonishingly good syrup may be made in advance and warmed for serving.

1 can (8¼ oz.) peaches   2 tbs. sugar
¼ cup orange juice   ¼ tsp. cinnamon
1½ tsp. cornstarch   ⅛ tsp. grated orange peel

Drain peaches and process in a blender container or food processor workbowl until smooth. Combine all ingredients in a small saucepan and heat over low heat, stirring often, until sauce has thickened. Simmer until you are ready to serve or allow to cool and refrigerate until needed.

LEMON CREAM

This topping is especially good. A "must try" with Yeasted Lemon Waffles, page 102, or any basic waffle.

4 oz. cream cheese, softened
¼ cup confectioners' sugar
1 tbs. lemon juice

½ tsp. grated lemon zest
1 tsp. poppy seeds, or to taste, optional

Cream softened cream cheese. Add remaining ingredients and mix until well-blended. Serve at room temperature or warmed in the microwave.

COCONUT DELIGHT

Serve with any tropical-type waffle or any waffle which contains coconut. Of course, it is absolutely delicious with a plain, basic waffle also.

½ cup canned coconut milk
¼ cup water

2 tsp. cornstarch
1 tbs. coconut flakes

Heat coconut milk, water and cornstarch over low heat until mixture thickens. Stir in coconut flakes until just mixed and remove from heat. Serve warm. Can be rewarmed in the microwave.

PIZZELLE FILLINGS

PIZZELLE FILLING IDEAS

Along with the delicious filling recipes in this chapter, consider any of the following purchased fillings or accompaniments to complement your pizzelle cookies:

- Cream of any flavor. Serve in bowls or waffle cones. Or, serve with a plain or chocolate-dipped pizzelle cookie as a garnish.
- Pudding of any flavor. If making pudding to complement a flavored pizzelle, add 1 tsp. of the same flavored extract to vanilla or chocolate pudding. To avoid soggy pizzelles, make pudding and allow to set before placing in bowl or cone.
- Fresh fruit and whipped cream. Move over, strawberry shortcake! Serve fresh sliced strawberries or any fresh fruit in a pizzelle bowl and top with whipped cream.
- No-bake pie fillings are a quick and easy bowl filling.
- Make or buy your favorite cracker dip and use it as a filling or dip with the *Herbed Parmesan Cheese Pizzelles*, page 131.
- Any favorite bagel topping such as lox and cream cheese can be served with *Herbed Parmesan Cheese Pizzelles*.

CHOCOLATE-DIPPED COOKIES

Serving a chocolate-dipped cylinder with coffee or ice cream is sure to be a treat. Roll cookies into cylinders or cut cookies into quarters immediately after removing from heat. Dip one end into the melted chocolate, sprinkle with chopped nuts or coconut if desired. Place on waxed paper to cool at room temperature.

To melt chocolate

Place 1 cup semisweet chocolate chips in a small microwave-proof bowl. Heat in the microwave, stirring every 30 seconds until melted. Or, heat over low heat, stirring until melted.

If dipping flavored pizzelles into chocolate, add 1 tsp. extract (orange, coconut, almond, mint, etc.) to 1 cup melted chocolate to complement the flavor of the pizzelle.

Examples:

Chocolate Coconut Pizzelle cylinders dipped in chocolate with coconut extract and sprinkled with shredded coconut.

Peppermint Pizzelle cylinders dipped in chocolate with mint extract and sprinkled with chopped nuts.

Orange Pizzelle cylinders dipped in chocolate with orange extract.

CREAMY PRESERVES

2 cups

Use any favorite preserves or marmalade. Apricot preserves goes with Almond Poppy Seed Pizzelles, page 125 for example. Orange marmalade goes really well with the Orange Cranberry Pizzelles, page 119, garnished with fresh mint leaves. Makes about 2 cups to stuff 1½ to 2 dozen cookies.

16 oz. cream cheese, softened
2 cups confectioners' sugar
1 tsp. vanilla extract
½ cup preserves or marmalade

Mix all ingredients together until creamy. Fill cylinders completely; see pages 110 and 111. Sprinkle chopped nuts on top of filling if desired. Refrigerate to set filling before serving.

CHOCOLATE-FRUIT-NUT FILLING

2 cups

Once again, fruit preserves are used to flavor this outstanding filling. This makes enough filling for 1 1/2 to 2 dozen cones or cylinders.

3 cups semisweet chocolate chips
1 cup fruit preserves
1/2 cup finely chopped nuts
1 tbs. vanilla or other flavor extract

Heat chocolate over low heat, stirring constantly until melted. Add fruit preserves, nuts and vanilla, mixing well. Fill cylinders completely. Place on plate or waxed paper and refrigerate to set filling.

Suggestions

Use raspberry or strawberry preserves in vanilla- or mint-flavored pizzelles.
Use orange preserves in orange- or mint-flavored pizzelles.

FLAVORED CREAM FILLING

2 cups

This is a superb filling for spiced pizzelles. Use the same flavor spice or seasoning in the filling as in the pizzelle. For example, a pumpkin pie-flavored cream filling with a pumpkin pie pizzelle cylinder makes a wonderful fall treat with hot cider! Makes enough to fill 1½ to 2 dozen cones or cylinders.

16 oz. cream cheese, softened	1 tbs. cinnamon, apple pie spice,
1 cup confectioners' sugar	pumpkin pie spice, nutmeg or
1 tsp. vanilla extract	allspice

Mix ingredients together until well blended. Fill cylinders or cones and refrigerate to set filling.

SAVORY FILLING

2 cups

This is a great savory filling for Herbed Parmesan Cheese Pizzelles, *page 131.*

16 oz. cream cheese, softened	2 tbs. parsley, chives or herb seasoning
1 cup butter, softened	blend

Mix ingredients together until well blended. Fill cylinders or cones and refrigerate to set filling, just a few minutes.

CANNOLI FILLING

While traditionally served in a Basic Sweet Cannoli (Pizzelle), *page 113, try* Honey Nut Oatmeal Pizzelles, *page 129, or a spiced pizzelle using the same spice as in the cannoli filling. This makes enough filling for 1½ to 2 dozen cannolis.*

1 lb. ricotta cheese
½ cup confectioners' sugar
⅓ cup granulated sugar
1 tsp. vanilla extract

¼ cup mini-chocolate chips
¼ cup finely chopped nuts (almonds, walnuts or pecans)

Beat together cheese, sugars and vanilla until mixture is stiff (about 8 to 10 minutes). Fold in mini-chocolate chips. Load pastry bag and fill shells completely. Press nuts into the ends. Refrigerate to set the filling, just a few minutes.

Suggested combinations

Use *Lemon* or *Orange Pizzelles,* pages 117 or 118, and add 1 tbs. lemon or orange zest to the filling mixture.

Use *Cinnamon Raisin Pizzelles,* page 120, or *Cinnamon Pecan Pizzelles,* page 132, and add 1 tsp. cinnamon to the filling mixture.

INDEX

Whipped cream waffles, yeasted
103
White chocolate macadamia nut
pizzelles 116
White chocolate waffles 23
White flour waffles
cottage cheese 24
Greek cheese and spinach 31
Mexican 30
potato 26
ricotta 24
sour cream 25
western 28
white chocolate 23
yogurt 24
Whole grain and cereal waffles
33–49
apple oatmeal 66
banana bran 41
buckwheat 40
buckwheat oatmeal 108
coconut rice 42
corn 38
granola 35
healthy whole grain 34
honey nut oatmeal 85
honey nut oatmeal, yeasted 101
oat bran 39
oatmeal 37
orange cinnamon oatmeal 62
rice 42

rye 43
Scandanavian rye 43
seven or nine grain 35
wheat flake 36
whole wheat 33
wild rice 42
whole wheat and bran, yeasted
107
Whole wheat and bran waffles,
yeasted 107
Whole wheat waffles 33
Wild rice waffles 42

Y
Yeasted waffles 98–108
about 98
basic 99
buckwheat oatmeal 108
Christmas morning 104
homestyle 106
honey nut oatmeal 101
lemon 102
orange nut 100
whipped cream 103
whole wheat and bran 107
Yogurt waffles 24

Serve Creative, Easy, Nutritious Meals with nitty gritty® Cookbooks

100 Dynamite Desserts
The 9 x 13 Pan Cookbook
The Barbecue Cookbook
Beer and Good Food
The Best Bagels are Made at Home
The Best Pizza is Made at Home
The Big Book of Bread Machine
    Recipes
Blender Drinks
Bread Baking
Bread Machine Cookbook
Bread Machine Cookbook II
Bread Machine Cookbook III
Bread Machine Cookbook IV
Bread Machine Cookbook V
Bread Machine Cookbook VI
Cappuccino/Espresso
Casseroles
The Coffee Book
Convection Oven Cookery
The Cook-Ahead Cookbook
Cooking for 1 or 2
Cooking in Clay

Cooking in Porcelain
Cooking on the Indoor Grill
Cooking with Chile Peppers
Cooking with Grains
Cooking with Your Kids
The Dehydrator Cookbook
Edible Pockets for Every Meal
Extra-Special Crockery Pot Recipes
Fabulous Fiber Cookery
Fondue and Hot Dips
Fresh Vegetables
From Freezer, 'Fridge and Pantry
From Your Ice Cream Maker
The Garlic Cookbook
Gourmet Gifts
Healthy Cooking on the Run
Healthy Snacks for Kids
The Juicer Book
The Juicer Book II
Lowfat American Favorites
New International Fondue Cookbook
No Salt, No Sugar, No Fat
One-Dish Meals

The Pasta Machine Cookbook
Pinch of Time: Meals in Less than 30
    Minutes
Quick and Easy Pasta Recipes
Recipes for the Loaf Pan
Recipes for the Pressure Cooker
Recipes for Yogurt Cheese
Risottos, Paellas, and other Rice
    Specialties
Rotisserie Oven Cooking
The Sandwich Maker Cookbook
The Sensational Skillet: Sautés and
    Stir-Fries
Slow Cooking in Crock-Pot,® Slow
    Cooker, Oven and Multi-Cooker
Soups and Stews
The Toaster Oven Cookbook
Unbeatable Chicken Recipes
The Vegetarian Slow Cooker
New Waffles and Pizzelles
The Well Dressed Potato
Wraps and Roll-Ups

For a free catalog, call: Bristol Publishing Enterprises, Inc.
(800) 346-4889
www.bristolcookbooks.com